THE ARDEN SHAKESPEARE

OTHELLO

EDITED BY

C. H. HERFORD, M.A., Litt.D.

PROFESSOR OF ENGLISH IN THE
UNIVERSITY OF MANCHESTER

REVISED BY

RAYMOND MacDONALD ALDEN

D. C. HEATH AND COMPANY

BOSTON	NEW YORK	CHICAGO
ATLANTA	SAN FRANCISCO	DALLAS
	LONDON	

GENERAL PREFACE

In this edition of SHAKESPEARE an attempt is made to present the greater plays of the dramatist in their literary aspect, and not merely as material for the study of philology or grammar. Criticism purely verbal and textual has only been included to such an extent as may serve to help the student in the appreciation of the essential poetry. Questions of date and literary history have been fully dealt with in the Introductions, but the larger space has been devoted to the interpretative rather than the matter-of-fact order of scholarship. Æsthetic judgments are never final, but the Editors have attempted to suggest points of view from which the analysis of dramatic motive and dramatic character may be profitably undertaken. In the Notes likewise, while it is hoped that all unfamiliar expressions and allusions have been adequately explained, yet it has been thought even more important to consider the dramatic value of each scene, and the part which it plays in relation to the whole. These general principles are common to the whole series; in detail each Editor is alone responsible for the play or plays that have been intrusted to him.

Every volume of the series has been provided with a Glossary, an Essay upon Metre, and an Index; and Appendices have been added upon points of special interest which could not conveniently be treated in the Introduction or the Notes. The text is based by the several Editors on that of the *Globe* edition.

CONTENTS

INTRODUCTION

SUMMARY

§ 1. Early performances. § 2. Texts. Comparison of Quarto and Folio. § 3. Date of composition. Character of style and rhythm.

§ 4. Cinthio's *Hecatommithi*. His story of the Moor of Venice. Summary. The historical background.

§ 5. What attracted Shakespeare in this story. Shakespearean tragedy. Character of the tragic hero. § 6. Application to *Othello*. Cinthio's story provided an opening for Shakespearean tragedy, but itself furnished scarcely the germ of it. § 7. Character of Othello. § 8. The betrayal of Cassio. Cassio's character. § 9. The nature of Othello's love. § 10. The betrayal of Desdemona. §11. From the temptation to the murder. §12. The character of Desdemona. § 13. The character of Iago. § 14. Emilia. § 15. Roderigo. § 16. Minor characters: Brabantio, Gratiano, Lodovico, the Duke and the Senator, Montano, Bianca, the Clown. § 17. Character of the action: its place among Shakespearean tragic plots. "Classical" character of action in Acts ii–v. The First Act and its relation to the sequel. § 18. Bearing of *Othello* upon our knowledge of Shakespeare's mind.

1. LITERARY HISTORY OF THE PLAY

§ 1. The first known performance of *Othello* was given by Shakespeare's company, the king's men, on November 1, 1604, before the Court, in the old Banqueting House at Whitehall.[1] It was from the first popular, and we have a record of two performances before illustrious visitors during Shakespeare's lifetime. On April 30, 1610, Prince Friedrich of Würtemberg, according to his secretary's journal, witnessed *l'histoire du More de Venise* at the Globe, *lieu ordinaire où l'on joue les comédies*. In February, 1613, it was one of the six dramas of Shakespeare played at the wedding festivities of the Princess Elizabeth. We may probably conclude from these data that *Othello* "held the stage continually" during Shakespeare's life (Lee, p. 389).

[1] This is established by the entry in the "Revells Booke" of 1605, a MS. volume covering the entries of 1604–5. The authenticity of this entry was for long uncertain, but is now definitively established. Cf. Lee, *Shakespeare*, p. 388, note.

§ 2. The play remained unpublished, however, till 1622, when one Thomas Walkley issued it in a Quarto edition with the title: The | Tragedy of Othello | The Moore of Venice. *As it hath beene diuerse times acted at the* | Globe, and at the Black-Friers, by | *his Maiesties Seruants.* | *Written by* William Shakespeare. | London. . . .

In the following year the play was printed in the First Folio edition of the entire works. In 1630 a Second Quarto was issued, and in 1655 a Third.

Of these texts the Third Quarto is merely a reprint of the Second, and has no independent value, while the Second represents the First with emendations founded upon the Folio text, which had appeared in the meantime. These "emendations" are sometimes right, but occasionally ignorant or stupid, and clearly have no claim to rest upon a Shakespearean tradition. There remain, therefore, only the First Quarto and the First Folio possessing rank as original sources.

Neither of these texts can be said to have a decisive superiority over the other, though that of the Folio is on the whole preferred. Each presents blunders and omissions not found in the other; each contributes undoubtedly Shakespearean matter which the other omits. A frequent source of difference is (1) in the *oaths*, certainly authentic, and reproduced in the Quarto, but excised, in accordance with the Act of Parliament, in the Folio; this makes probable that the Quarto was printed from a MS. which had long ceased to be used in the theater, and may not be much later than the original performance of the play. Even expressions like *God's will*, *Zounds* (God's wounds), and *by the mass* are omitted or replaced by innocent formulæ like *in troth* in the Folio. All these phrases are, of course, restored from the Quarto in modern texts. (2) The language of the Quarto is in general rather more colloquial and nearer to the actual pronunciation of the time; thus *ha* is often given for *have*, not only where it is slurred, as in

I *ha* bin to-night exceedingly well cudgelled (ii. 3. 371),

but where it carries a strong emphasis, e.g.

How poor are they that *ha* not patience! (ii. 3. 375).

The Folio regularly substitutes *have*. Similarly, *bin* for *been*, *has* for *hath*, *ifaith* for *in faith*, and forms like *he'll 't is*, *'t was*, &c., preponderate in the Quarto, the fuller forms in the Folio. The Quarto occasionally uses the colloquial (and archaic) *em* for *them*. The fatal *handkerchief* is regularly given by the Quarto in the colloquial form *handkercher*. But most of the contracted or colloquial forms also occur in the Folio, and the uncontracted in the Quarto, even when the latter are metrically required, as in iii. 3. 313:

> *Emilia.* Look, here 't is.   *Iago.* A good wench; give it me.

So, the Folio used the form *Desdemon*, where strict scansion requires, for the full name; the rather archaic *twiggen* for the Quarto *wicker*, in ii. 3. 152, and the colloquial *mam'ring* (mammering), iii. 3. 72, for the Quarto *muttering*.

(3) In a number of cases the Quarto reading is replaced by one clearly superior in the Folio; in a smaller number of others the Folio reading is inferior. Examples of the first kind are (from a single scene):—

ii. 3. 193, F.

> your name is great
> In *mouths* of wisest censure.   (Q 1, *men*.)

ii. 3. 206, F.

> passion having my best judgment *collied*.   (Q 1, *cooled*.)

ii. 3. 221, F.

> I had rather have this tongue *cut from* my mouth.
>   (Q 1, *out from*, whence Q 2, *out of*.)

ii. 3. 139, F.

> his good nature
> *Prizes* the virtue that appears in Cassio.
>   (Q 1, *praises*.)

Examples of the second:—

i. 1. 101, Q 1.

> Upon malicious *bravery*.   (F, *knavery*.)

ii. 1. 267, Q 1.

> when these *mutualities* so marshal the way.
>   (F, *mutabilities*.)

iv. 2. 55, Q.

> A fixed figure for the time of scorn
> To point his slow *unmoving* finger(s) at!
>   (F, *and moving*.)

As the last example shows, the Folio and the Quarto may each be more authentic for particular words or phrases in the same passage; thus *finger* (Folio), not *fingers* (Quarto), is clearly right. A striking instance of a passage thus constructed by modern editors from materials furnished by Quarto and Folio, but not itself as a whole found anywhere, is i. 3. 375 (the parting between Iago and Roderigo at the close of the Senate scene). The old texts are here verbally reproduced.

Q 1 has:

> *Iag.* Go to, farewell:—doe you heare *Roderigo?*
> *Rod.* What say you?
> *Iag.* No more of drowning, doe you heare?
> *Rod.* I am chang'd.   [*Exit Roderigo.*
> *Iag.* Goe to, farewell, put money enough in your purse:
>   Thus doe I ever make my foole my purse.

F 1 has:

> *Iago.* Go too, farewel. Do you heare *Roderigo?*
> *Rod.* I'll sell all my land.   [*Exit.*
> *Iago.* Thus do I ever make my Foole, my purse.

Q 2, correcting Q 1 by F 1, combines these thus:

> *Iago.* Go to, farewell:—doe you heare *Roderigo?*
> *Rod.* What say you?
> *Iago.* No more of drowning, doe you heare?
> *Rod.* I am chang'd: Ile goe sell all my land. [*Exit.*
> *Iago.* Thus doe I ever make my foole my purse.

This is followed substantially by the Cambridge and other modern editions.

(4) Finally, the Folio contains a number of passages (totalling about one hundred and sixty lines) not found in the Quarto, and the Quarto about a dozen lines in all not found in the Folio. The chief longer passages of the first class are the following:—i. 1. 122–38; i. 2. 72–7; i. 3. 24–30; iii. 3. 383–90; iii. 3. 453–60; iv. 1. 38–44; iv. 2. 151–64; iv. 3. 31–53; iv. 3. 87–104; v. 2. 185–93; *ib.* 266–72.

It is not doubted that all these passages, as well as those peculiar to the Quarto, were written by Shakespeare. But the question arises whether the passages found only in the Folio were parts of the original text omitted in the Quarto, or whether they were Shakespeare's "afterthoughts," which do not appear in the Quarto merely because it reproduces the original MS., in which they did not occur. Dr. A. C. Bradley, to whom the above list is due, has examined all these passages, with a result which permits us to dismiss the second hypothesis.[1] In the great majority of cases the passage is more or less closely bound up with the context; two or three (e.g. Emilia's reflections on husbands, iv. 3. 87 f.) are obvious "cuts." Several can only be explained as printer's omissions in the Quarto; only in two or three is insertion by afterthought even conceivable.

The conclusions made probable from the above evidence are that both texts (Q 1 and F 1) were printed from substantially authentic copies of the play. That Q 1 was printed from an early acting

[1] *Shakespearean Tragedy*, Appendix, Note J.

version, with some cuts and blunders, aggravated by careless printing, but here and there preserving an authentic phrase of which the tradition would otherwise have been lost. That F 1 was printed from a MS. much nearer, on the whole, to the author's text, restoring most of the "cuts," but here and there itself slightly curtailed, and in a number of cases "corrected" without authority, and for the worse. Whether its somewhat more modern and "literary" English is a restoration of Shakespeare's writing, or regulation of it by the fashions of 1623, must be left uncertain.

§ 3. The well-authenticated date of the first performance of *Othello* (November 1, 1604) probably followed its completion by a few months at most. In time sequence, as well as in tragic character, it forms a group with *Hamlet*, which certainly preceded (Q 1, 1603; Q 2, 1604), and *King Lear* and *Macbeth*, which certainly followed (1605–6). *Measure for Measure*, performed a few weeks later at Whitehall, was also probably the work of 1604, and may be regarded as the most nearly contemporary with *Othello* of all the plays.[1] The "tests" of verse, and the subtler tests of style, confirm the close chronological connection of these five plays, and though they are very insecure guides in determining the order of plays within the same group, or otherwise separated by short intervals of time, they at least offer nothing inconsistent with the position assigned to *Othello*, after *Hamlet* and before *Lear* and *Macbeth*. Shakespeare had now reached, after ten or twelve years of continuous dramatic artistry, a style of consummate dramatic quality. The decorative and lyrical excesses of his earlier writing, the "taffeta phrases" which ravished him no less than they did the lords of Navarre, the linked sweetness of rhymes, even of stanzas and sonnets in dialogue, to which he had returned (as in *Midsummer-Night's Dream* and *Romeo and Juliet*) from the austerer example of Marlowe—all these exuberances of young genius were now subdued to the needs of dramatic expression. There are far more fine phrases in *Hamlet* than in *Love's Labour's Lost*, but they are steeped in the mind of the Prince or the passion of Ophelia; and although rhymes appear in *Othello*, conveying a string of platitudes or an epigram, they are employed to accentuate the sententious gravity of the Duke, or the sardonic irony of Brabantio or Iago. And when the same dramatic need calls, Shakespeare can now be utterly simple, as he can now imagine characters of utter simplicity. The princess of France and her ladies would

---

[1] Adams suggests that "while reading Cinthio's *Hecatommithi* in preparation for *Measure for Measure*, Shakespeare came upon the narrative of the Moor." (*Life of Shakespeare*, p. 363.)

have blushed to utter a sentence so devoid of brilliant point as Desdemona's

I am very sorry that you are not well (iii. 3. 289),

and Shakespeare himself would then as certainly have rejected it, had he as yet been capable of conceiving womanhood of this exquisite *naïveté*. But a certain noble plainness, passing without effort into magnificence, is the characteristic of the style of *Othello*, among the tragedies, as it is, notably, of the speech of the great Moor himself— the speech of a man grandly simple in make and habit of mind, but with sudden splendors of transfiguring poetry. The tragic intensity of the third and fourth acts, in particular, is conveyed through language, for Shakespeare, almost strikingly unadorned, as if the sheer force of situation made the luxuries of speech superfluous and irrelevant. But ever and anon the pervading economy breaks down before the romantic imagination of Othello, or the penetrating intellect of Iago, and the language takes on the splendid or close-knit habit of their minds. There is no question here of "rhetorical excrescences." Every one of the enthralling poetic outbursts is dramatically justified. In the union of complete dramatic plasticity with consummate poetic reach lies the principal characteristic of Shakespeare's maturest style. *Othello* marks perhaps its culminating point; in any case, its stylistic character is in keeping with the chronological position assigned to it on other grounds, near the middle of the "tragic period."

2. SOURCE OF THE PLOT

§ 4. Shakespeare found the story in the collection, long familiar to him and to his dramatic colleagues, called the *Hecatommithi* ("Hundred Tales"), by Giraldi Cinthio. Giovanibattista Giraldi Cinthio was Professor of Philosophy at Ferrara, and an active and prolific man of letters, who holds a distinguished place among the Italian dramatists of the Renaissance.

In the "Hundred Tales," as in the *Decameron* ("Ten Days") of his master Boccaccio, the stories do not succeed one another with the seeming (but artfully contrived) disorder of the *Canterbury Tales*, but are arranged in groups according to type of subject. The general topic of the Third Decade, to which our story (iii. 7) belongs, is "the unfaithfulness of husbands and wives." It may be summarized as follows. With the exception of the heroine ("Disdemona"), none of the persons are named. The complete text, with a translation, is given in Hazlitt's *Shakespeare's Library* and Furness's New Variorum edition.

Summary

1. The Moor, a soldier of distinction, living at Venice, and in high regard there, is loved by Disdemona, a lady of noble character and beauty, and returns her love. They are married, against the will of her relatives, and live together in perfect concord.

2. The Venetian government, happening to change the garrison at Cyprus, appointed the Moor commander of the fresh troops; Disdemona, at her urgent entreaty, was allowed to accompany him. Among his soldiers was an ensign, in high favor with the Moor, a man of great personal beauty, but of the most depraved nature in the world. There was also a captain, much beloved by the Moor, whom, as her husband's friend, Disdemona, too, treats with the greatest kindness. She was also friendly with the ensign's wife.

3. The ensign fell passionately in love with Disdemona, and finding all his efforts vain, ascribed his failure to her being in love with the captain, and plotted to convict her of adultery. But the Moor's love for his wife and friendship for the captain were such that he could only succeed by stratagem.

4. Some time after the captain was degraded for striking a soldier; Disdemona did her utmost to induce the Moor to restore him, and the Moor told the ensign that he feared her importunity would force him to comply. From this hint the ensign took his cue, and suggested that Disdemona might have reasons for her favor. The Moor asked for explanation, but was merely told to use his eyes. When she next pleaded for the captain, he took her sharply to task. But the ensign, pressed to produce evidence, could only insinuate that she was repelled by his blackness.

5. The ensign accordingly tried to strengthen his case. He contrived to abstract from her person, while she dandled his child, a handkerchief, given by Othello, and left it in the captain's chamber. For some days Disdemona did not miss it. The captain, finding it, and knowing it to be hers, came to her house to restore it. As he knocked, the Moor returned home and the captain fled. The Moor, his suspicions confirmed, called for the handkerchief, on which Disdemona, reddening, pretended to hunt for it, and at last asked feebly whether he had not taken it himself. But the Moor still wished to see the handkerchief actually in the captain's possession. The ensign arranged this, taking the Moor past the captain's house, where his lady, a virtuoso in embroidery, was copying the work.

6. The Moor, now wholly convinced, plans with the ensign the death of the captain and Disdemona. The ensign is afraid of the captain and requires to be bribed. The captain, one evening, is wounded in the leg. Disdemona, the next morning, hears the news with grief. The ensign proposes a plan for Disdemona's death. Some days after they carry it out, beating her to death with a stocking filled with sand, and then screen themselves by pulling down

a beam from the ceiling and give out that she was killed by its fall.

7. After Disdemona's burial the Moor grieves for her. But the ensign incenses the captain against him, and together they bring against the Moor accusations that lead to his being recalled to Venice, tortured, and banished. He is ultimately slain by Disdemona's kin. The ensign continues his malpractices and is ultimately put to death for a wholly unconnected offence.

8. The whole story is supposed to be told by the ensign's wife, who was cognizant of her husband's plot, but was cowed by fear of him from revealing it.

We may note, without comment at this stage, the most obvious points in which the story differs from the play.

1. The action is *leisurely*. The Moor and Disdemona have lived together at Venice for some time before the intrigue begins. There are also repeated intervals of "several days" in its course.

2. The ensign "loves" Disdemona, believes that she loves the captain, and takes the vengeance of a foiled suitor upon both.

3. His wife is cognizant of his plot.

4. A new character appears in the "donna" in the captain's house, who is eager to copy the embroidery of the handkerchief, and is seen by the Moor copying it; while Shakespeare's Bianca, representing the courtesan with whom the captain goes to supper, angrily refuses to copy it.

5. The death of Disdemona and the sequel are entirely different.

6. The political and military background are almost wholly wanting. Shakespeare has made the historic attack of the Turks upon Cyprus in 1570 (subsequent to the publication of Cinthio's story) the outward occasion of the whole action.

3. CRITICAL APPRECIATION

§ 5. What drew Shakespeare to this story of sordid intrigue and stupid crime as material for tragic drama? We must begin by asking what tragic drama now, in 1604, meant for Shakespeare. Little as we know of the ways of his mind, we are justified in holding that from about 1601 to about 1608, while he was shaping the four supreme tragedies and the three only less wonderful Roman plays, his imagination was dominated by a certain ideal of tragic effect which he achieved, with endless diversity in detail, by certain common procedures of art. This ideal and these procedures were the source of what we call "Shakespearean tragedy" *par excellence*. How Shakespeare himself would have described it we can only guess. But in our terms it meant, stripped of less important features, the ruin and death of a man of extraordinary greatness and intensity of soul by the concurrence of an outward, usually hostile, situation with some weakness or blindness rooted in his own character, and often directly derived from his noblest and most splendid traits.

Previous Elizabethan tragedy presented some features of this tragic scheme rough-hewn. The "one-man play," where the interest is concentrated on a tragic hero struggling with a host of enemies, was traditional. He might be a noble-minded man in conflict with criminals, as in the avenger-plays. Or he might be a man of towering force, swayed by a single passion or motive, like Tamburlaine. More often he was himself criminal as well as immensely able, like Barabbas. The only pre-Shakespearean hero of tragedy who is tragic in the full Shakespearean sense is Faustus.

Where Shakespeare in his conception of tragedy went beyond his predecessors (and his own early efforts) was, above all, in the character of the hero. The lofty and noble spirit, burdened with some temperamental weakness or blindness which, precisely in the situation he is brought into, proves ruinous and fatal, was not perhaps Shakespeare's discovery, for it is Greek in essence; but no one had yet disclosed to the full the sublimity and pathos possible in tragedy thus brought about. For such a hero cannot be hated. In our horror even of Macbeth's crimes there mingles admiration for his splendid qualities and pity for his illusions. The complete sympathy which all his tragic heroes excite—rising, in a Hamlet or an Othello, to a passion of grief and love—is one of the hall-marks of Shakespearean tragedy, and a chief source of its purifying and uplifting power.

The union of great power with weakness can, of course, take many forms. The case which seems to have most strongly appealed to Shakespeare was that of the man of native grandeur of mind, who, in his intercourse with more ordinary men, is in some way blinded and baffled by the large scale on which he feels and thinks. His blindness may look like folly, but it is a folly rooted in his greatness. He appears impracticably generous, like Brutus, or childishly credulous, like Timon and Lear, or childishly obsessed with his own prowess, like Coriolanus. But not all Shakespeare's tragic heroes are of this type. In Macbeth and Antony we find a no less towering grandeur of mind. The errors which bring about their tragic doom are not, however, the guileless blunders of noble simplicity, but vices of lawless passion. While in the case of Hamlet, finally, an idealist equally free from the *naïveté* of the first group and from the viciousness of the second, the tragic doom is brought about by the unnerving melancholy into which he is plunged by his loathing for his mother's sin. In so far as this springs not from any weakness of character, but from his noble idealism itself, he resembles the "Brutus" group; whereas his intellectual maturity and self-possession ally him rather to Antony and Macbeth—sometimes described as a "criminal Hamlet."

In all these cases the hero is the undoubted focus of the tragic interest. In *Hamlet* this is proverbial. But it is equally certain in *Macbeth* and *Antony and Cleopatra*, where another character approaches the hero very closely in importance and interest, or in *Julius Cæsar*, where the "hero" is not the nominal subject of the play at all. What, then, was the part of the action in relation to this central figure? Certain types of action, no less than certain types of character, would be better fitted than others for bringing about the tragic issue and the tragic effect. An ideal tragic action would be one which would give full scope to the hero's greatness and bring his defects disastrously into play. It would be related to him somewhat as a key to the wards of a lock. The Ghost's summons finds its way to the weakness of Hamlet, and lets loose the tragic doom; put Macbeth's Witches in the place of the Ghost, the key would not have fitted, and the door would have remained closed. Without Cassius at his elbow, Brutus would not have wrecked the conspiracy.

§ 6. In the foregoing survey of Shakespearean tragedy our present play has been deliberately left out of account. To it we must now return. How is *Othello* related to the other mature tragedies? That the hero belongs to our first group, the grand-simple type of Timon and Lear, is evident; he is perhaps its most perfect example. The great distinctive feature of this drama, among the mature tragedies, lies not in the hero, magnificent creation as he is, but in the external agency by which the tragic situation is brought about. Cassius, and Lady Macbeth, and Cleopatra, the Weird Sisters, and the Ghost, play, of course, a large part in thrusting the hero into the situation which is to prove tragic for him and them; but none of them, like Iago, *invents* a situation which becomes tragic because the hero supposes it real. It is as if Lady Macbeth had persuaded her husband that the gentle Duncan was a traitor, and Macbeth had slain him by way of just vengeance. Tragedy thus resting upon invention, upon make-believe, inevitably wants something of the weighty substance which belongs to the tragic clash of real and significant world-forces, as in *Antigone;* and this is part of the reason why *Othello* does impress us as, in substance, somehow slighter than

Hamlet or *Lear*. On the other hand, no tragedy is more acutely pathetic than that which arises from a fatal misunderstanding; and in this kind of tragedy *Othello* is unequalled in Shakespearean drama.

What opening, then, did Cinthio's story offer for such tragedy as this? Simply the outline of an intrigue and a catastrophe, ingeniously managed, but without a hint of greatness. The Moor is merely gross and simple. The ensign meanly avenges himself for his rejection by his commandant's wife. He is at bottom a coward, and has to be encouraged by a bribe. His own wife is a feeble accomplice. Disdemona herself alone offers a suggestion of pathos. All the persons, save the heroine, are cast in a petty mould, and the story itself is an ordinary barrack-room scandal of the day, passably well told. The whole creative, transforming work remained for Shakespeare to do.

§ 7. The critical problem clearly lay in the character of Othello. Was it possible for a man who is thus grossly deceived to be great—so great that his ruin is tragic? To be great even in being deceived, great even when he is destroying his innocent wife? For an Othello who should fulfil these conditions, some kinds of greatness, at least, were ruled out. He could not have the penetrating intelligence of Hamlet, nor his infallible insight into men. But he might have the magnanimity of Brutus, and be wrecked by noble blunders, like him. And this, if not the only solution, was certainly the most Shakespearean. It was, in any case, the one which Shakespeare chose.

Othello is, then, a man at once grandly and simply built, towering in sheer force and nobility above all who surround him. He knows his strength, but has not a particle of arrogance. He neither vaunts his services nor affects to disdain them. He wins recognition and deference with the spontaneous ease of power. He masters without hesitation or effort every situation he is confronted with—save only that which is expressly arranged to delude him by the deliberate devilry of Iago. It is not merely that he always finds the right words and the effective way; there is a magic in his speech and manner, which, backed by his compelling force of personality, masters the prejudices of exclusive Venice, and kindles in sensitive spirits like Cassio and Desdemona an ardor of devotion. Even her father "loves" him, and listens as gladly as she to his tales of "moving accidents by flood and field." He is a soldier; Venice confides in his prowess; war is his "occupation" and delight, and he quits with anguish its "glorious pomp and circumstance." But no soldier (least of all the greatest of Shakespearean soldiers, Coriolanus) ever knew better when force is out of place.

His very first words are a gentle reproof of Iago's professed wish "to have yerk'd [Brabantio] here under the ribs":

> 'T is better as it is.

Presently, it is he who calls the civil brawlers to keep the peace:

> Keep up your bright swords, for the dew will rust them.

And then:

> Were it my cue to fight, I should have known it
> Without a prompter.

And with what admirable temper he meets old Brabantio's furious order to carry him off to prison:

> What if I do obey?
> How may the duke be therewith satisfied . . .?

Of Othello in his proper "occupation" of war, our glimpses are few but sufficient. "The man commands like a full soldier," is the admiring tribute of those who have served under him, like Montano (ii. 1. 35). When summoned to "slubber the gloss of his new fortunes" with the "more stubborn and boisterous expedition" to Cyprus, he puts aside the good-natured condolence of the duke, not like a man resolutely accepting a hard duty, newly-married lover though he is, but with a kind of eager joy:

> The tyrant custom, most grave senators,
> Hath made the flinty and steel couch of war
> My thrice-driven bed of down; I do agnize
> A natural and prompt alacrity
> I find in hardness.   (i. 3. 230 f.)

But this man, so easily secure in every other situation, falls, almost without resistance, into the gross trap prepared for him by Iago. He is, in short, simply as well as grandly built. His simplicity is that of one who thinks too largely to apprehend easily the devices and subterfuges natural to weaker and smaller men. Such simplicity goes well, as we have seen, with the heroic character, but it is clearly distinguished from everything that at all resembles it elsewhere in Shakespeare. The simplicity of Coriolanus is the mere obtuseness of the great fighter who scorns all arts and accomplishments but those of the camp. The simplicity of Lear is the blindness of a lifelong autocrat who has read the world only through an elusive veil of flattery and subservience. The simplicity of Brutus is the too abstract habit of a doctrinaire mind, plunged without preparation into the welter of politics. The case of Brutus is least unlike the case of Othello, for in both men it is something great and ideal in them, their very magnanimity, that betrays them, whereas with Coriolanus and Lear, grand as they are, what works disaster is something childish and futile. But the mind of Brutus, with all his philosophic culture, appears narrow, even provincial, beside the magnificent amplitude and intensity of Othello, the nursling of deserts and battle-fields; as Brutus's finest eloquence appears pedestrian beside the enthralling poetry that breaks at every decisive moment, unsought, from Othello's lips.

Such a man might, perhaps, have in any case found himself at a disadvantage in a city reputed to be inhabited by the most astute and subtle population in Europe. But Othello is further distinguished from the Venetians by race, by color, by cast of experience. Whether—beyond the "thick-lips" (i. 1. 67), and the swarthy complexion[1]—Shakespeare associated any racial traits with his "Moor," as he certainly did with his French (*Henry V*) and Welsh (*Henry IV*), is doubtful. That "these Moors are changeable in their wills" (i. 3. 352) no doubt expresses a current opinion about them in England. But Iago's gibes must not be taken to be part of the characterization of Othello. Iago himself, when alone, gives the lie to this sneer, admitting that the Moor is likely to prove constant in love (ii. 1. 298). It will not do, in any case, to imagine that Othello himself is seriously contrasted as a noble barbarian with the refined civility of Venice; in fine breeding he is fully a match for the most polished Venetian he meets. But that he is racially distinct from the Venetians, an alien in the society which accepts him in its own interest, and into which he has married, is a fact of moment for the plot. Iago subtly uses it to insinuate his ignorance of the crafty ways of Venetian women. Brabantio loved him and invited him; but that his daughter should "leap," even by way of marriage, "into the sooty bosom" of this alien is too monstrous to have been effected without illicit "charms." And this alien soldier has come

[1] It is interesting to recall that Othello's color was one of the reasons employed by Lamb in his paradoxical argument that the tragedies of Shakespeare are unfitted for presentation on the visible stage. Desdemona's love for a black man, he said, is the triumph "of imagination over the senses"; but in the theater, "left to our poor unassisted senses," we find it revolting. See also, in Furness's New Variorum edition, pp. 389–96, a number of arguments on the question whether Othello should be represented on the modern stage as a black man.

to Venice, nine months before the play opens, from a life of romantic and mysterious adventure. He is born of men of "royal siege"; from his seventh year he has travelled and fought and suffered "by flood and field," in "antres vast and deserts idle," among cannibals and in enemy prisons. He has seen men whose heads do grow beneath their shoulders, and received a magic handkerchief from an eastern sibyl. His life is a romance, and Desdemona was not the only Venetian listener whom it enthralled. He is obviously admired "for the dangers he has passed," as well as prized in the interest of the general safety. But neither such admiration nor the friendly regard he doubtless gave in return could yield the intimate understanding founded on common blood.

Iago perfectly appreciates all these points. Even before he has conceived his plot he can scoff, as we have seen, at the frailty of love vows taken by a pair so ill-mated, and his scoff is too cynical not to express his mind. And the thought that clinches his resolve when his plot is shaped is that:

> The Moor is of a free and open nature,
> That thinks men honest that but seem to be so,
> And will as tenderly be led by the nose
> As asses are. (i. 3. 405.)

In working this "free open nature," deeply as he despises it, Iago proceeds with extraordinary astuteness. He prepares the ground with the utmost care; fortune, moreover, plays into his hands. Before breathing any suspicion of Desdemona herself, he suggests a suspicion of Cassio, his lieutenant. It was an easy and safe first step, which, successfully taken, the further enterprise would be comparatively simple. And Cassio's character lends itself to his cunning strategy.

§ 8. Some circumstances were indeed against him. As in the novel, Cassio is the Moor's intimate and trusted friend; until the moment of dismissal he is always "Michael" to his chief. He is, indeed, a man of singular charm; outwardly engaging ("a proper man"), and with "a daily beauty in his life" which Iago, frankest of cynics, fears to have set beside the "ugliness" of his own (v. 1. 19). But these engaging qualities only serve to bring Cassio into the kind of ambiguous situation required for Iago's purpose. He is attractive to women, and himself easily inflamed by their charm. Iago's "almost damned in a fair wife" probably conveys this in his coarse dialect. The light o' love, Bianca, whom other men pursue, runs piteously after him to implore him to return (iv. 4. 172 f.). Othello

had used his persuasive tongue to plead his cause with Desdemona;
Cassio had "gone a-wooing with him" and carried messages "very
oft" between them (iii. 3, 70, 94, 100).[1] It is clear, too, that, in
the conduct of this delicate business, Cassio has conceived a wor-
shipping adoration of the exquisite character of Desdemona, while
she gives him warm friendship in return. There was as little thought
of disloyalty on his part as on hers; but both were naturally frank,
she through innocence, he by his ardent and impulsive temperament.[2]
Iago was not present when Cassio, awaiting the arrival of her ship
with his men on the Cyprus shore, breaks into that lyric ecstasy of
admiration of "the divine Desdemona," a maid

> That paragons description and wild fame.

But he witnessed their meeting, with its confidences, handclasps,
and other signs of warm friendship; and "with as little a web as
this will I ensnare as great a fly as Cassio" (ii. 1. 169).

Iago accordingly proceeds to take the first step—the night brawl.
His conduct of the business, a brilliant piece of acting in every
point (cf. § 13), and especially his "report" to Othello, shows that
he is at least as much concerned to convince Othello that he is
Cassio's good friend as to secure his dismissal. Both are necessary
to his plot. It would have seriously discounted the second success,
and his use of Desdemona's consequent pleading for her friend's
reinstatement, had Othello had reason to suspect him of paying
off a grudge against Cassio—nay, against himself. Yet there was
good ground for such suspicion; Othello had just given the lieu-
tenancy to Cassio, passing over Iago. Was it so certain that this
Venetian, who had seen a Florentine appointed over his head in
the Venetian service by a general who was also an alien, would
neglect a chance of paying off his grudge on both by embroiling
them in a groundless quarrel? Such a situation would have put
a wary man on his guard. But nothing of the kind occurs to Othello.

Iago, however, was conscious of the risk, and exerts himself to

---

[1] In i. 2. 50 f., it is true, Cassio appears to hear of the marriage,
and even of Desdemona, for the first time. We must suppose either
that, being in the secret of the elopement, he feigns ignorance, or,
with Dr. Bradley, that Shakespeare later introduced the circumstance of Cassio's cognizance of the courtship, seeing its importance
for the plot, and omitted to make the requisite alteration here.

[2] The difference between his loyal and delicate sense of Desdemona's
charm and Iago's gross estimate of a woman "full of game" is finely
touched in the little dialogue between them (ii. 3. 15–29).

appear as Cassio's good friend, who would do his utmost to shield him from punishment. He succeeds completely.

> I know, Iago,
> Thy honesty and love doth mince the matter,
> Making it light to Cassio.

Clearly, after this, Iago could reckon with some security that his graver insinuation against Cassio would also be regarded by Othello as the unwilling testimony of a good friend, not as the calumny of a disappointed rival.

But Iago had also secured his main point, Cassio's dismissal, and he now proceeds to build upon it the opening situation of his plot. Desdemona's compassionate sympathy for her friend in his sudden disgrace might be trusted to hurry her to imprudent lengths; but Iago, who leaves no stone unturned, works further upon her eager, impressionable nature by feigning himself grieved, and conveying this to her through his wife:

> O, that 's an honest fellow. Do not doubt, Cassio,
> But I will have my lord and you again
> As fixedly as you were. (iii. 3. 5.)

Her unreasonable importunity in the ensuing passage fulfilled Iago's calculation completely. What his gross nature hardly foresaw was that Cassio, in his self-abasement, would shrink away from the presence of his old commander, and thus put the deadliest of weapons in Iago's hands.

> *Oth.* Was not that Cassio parted from my wife?
> *Iago.* Cassio, my lord! No, sure, I cannot think it,
> That he would steal away so guilty-like,
> Seeing you coming. (iii. 3. 37 *f.*)

The ground at all points thus prepared, Iago's case against Cassio is established almost before it is stated. He has only to hint his suspicion, and the momentum of his authority, as one not only "full of love and honesty," but who weighs his words before he gives them breath, drives it home more surely than explicit proof. His very "stops" and hesitations "fright me the more," cries the unhappy victim.

Iago's hints take Othello utterly unawares. Just because he had never dreamed of asking whether this charming officer, his confidential go-between, could possibly be disloyal, he became the more helpless to resist the doubt when it was suggested by another friend, who was also Cassio's friend, and whose honesty was a proverb.

The same terrible power of obsession serves Iago in the more delicate and hazardous operation of incriminating Desdemona. But before discussing this it is necessary to consider the nature of Othello's love.

§ 9. Othello is not prone to love, as he is not prone to suspect evil. At the time of the action, too, he is no longer young, and the first ardor of masculine passion has subsided (i. 3. 264). He even speaks of himself as having declined into the vale of years ("though that's not much"), and fears that this may be the explanation of his young wife's infidelity (iii. 3. 265). And as for marriage, he has prized his life of roving adventure and "unhoused freedom" so dearly that he would not "for the sea's worth" have put it into the "circumscription and confines" of a home, but that he "loved the gentle Desdemona" (i. 2. 24 f.). Nay, he loved her, he tells us himself, because she "pitied" the incidental hardships of this roving life. He is conscious of surrendering something in marriage. None the less, Desdemona had touched the springs of a passion which takes possession of him like a transfiguring flame, and sweeps all considerations of gain or loss to the winds. It stirs that which is rarest and most wonderful in him, the imaginative vision and ecstasy of a poet. It did not, indeed, need imagination to find in Shakespeare's Desdemona the crowning marvel of his romantic career. But this apparition of exquisite womanhood, discovered in the heart of a mundane population, enchants him the more because its loveliness has, with all its engaging reality, the rarity and strangeness of romance. Her beauty ravishes him with a poignancy which no mere acuteness of the senses could produce.

> O thou weed,
> Who art so lovely fair and smell'st so sweet
> That the sense aches at thee. (iv. 2. 68.)

> Yet I'll not shed her blood,
> Nor scar that whiter skin of hers than snow,
> And smooth as monumental alabaster. (v. 2. 3.)

Again and again her visible presence, suddenly entering, or her appealing glance, drives back the forces of malign suggestion. When he has stabbed her with the words, "Heaven truly knows that thou art false as hell," and she asks, "To whom, my lord? with whom? how am I false?" he bursts into tears:

> O Desdemona! away! away! away! (iv. 2. 39.)

And before the crisis of the last scene:

> Ah, balmy breath, that dost almost persuade
> Justice to break her sword! (v. 2. 17.)

So potent was the spell of Desdemona's presence when his mind was already poisoned against her. What it was to him before it had to contend with this malign influence, we know from the ineffable cry of rapture—not less a cry that it is uttered in perfectly measured speech—with which he meets her at Cyprus:

> O my soul's joy!
> If after every tempest come such calms,
> May the winds blow till they have waken'd death!
>
> .   .   .   .
>
>   If it were now to die,
> 'T were now to be most happy; for I fear
> My soul hath her content so absolute
> That not another comfort like to this
> Succeeds in unknown fate.

In these and other passages Othello expresses the spiritual exaltation of love with an intensity nowhere surpassed in literature. And so completely does his joy in Desdemona answer to the feelings which Shakespeare's portrayal of her rouses in us, that we imagine that he knows her as we know her. Yet, a few hours after this rapturous meeting, he believes she has grossly betrayed him, and murders her in her bed. His words seem to reflect a sense of the loveliness of Desdemona's nature beyond the power of all Iago's strategy to disturb. And yet a few halting sentences suffice to shatter it. How explain this paradox?

The truth is that Othello's love has all the traits of a deep and noble passion save one—insight into the soul of the woman he loves. That love is "blind" was proverbial; but what Othello is blind to, or only insecurely sees, is not her faults, but her childlike purity of nature. Had he seen it, he could not have been persuaded that it was not there. He has momentary glimpses of it, but they pass with her presence, and finally her presence itself fails to evoke them:

> If she be false, oh then Heaven mocks itself!
> I'll not believe it.   (iii. 3. 98.)

What he does see, and describes with intense poetry of feeling and phrase, is not her soul, but the emotion with which her apparition fills his own. What he *knows* with absolute clearness, and feels with overwhelming power, is not that she is true, but that he cannot live if she be false.

> There when I have garner'd up my heart,
> Where either I must live or bear no life;
> The fountain from the which my being runs
> Or else dries up—to be discarded thence.
>
>   (iv. 2. 57 *f.*)

And he knows this even before he has conceived a doubt of her truth. Witness his outburst when she has left him at the outset of the Temptation scene:

> Excellent wretch! Perdition catch my soul
> But I do love thee! and when I love thee not,
> Chaos is come again. (iii. 3. 90 *f.*)

§ 10. It was with a lover and husband of this quality that Iago had to do. Of the depth and the romantic beauty of Othello's love his foul mind could have no conception, but he perfectly understood how little it sprang from secure knowledge. He had observed and noted, too, all the incidental circumstances which favored the attempt to wreck it. He was shrewd enough, indeed, to see that Othello was of a "noble and loving nature," and that to destroy his love was an immensely formidable task. He approached it accordingly with extraordinary circumspection and subtlety in the crucial portion of the Temptation scene. Up to iii. 3. 110, at least, Othello has no suspicion of his wife. Cassio, he supposes, has made improper advances to her, but of her complicity there is as yet no question. But Iago now stealthily creates the impression that there is some darker mystery behind, some monster in his thought too hideous to be shown. His hesitations, his half sentences ("For Michael Cassio, I dare be sworn that he is honest" [but—]), and finally, his resolute, even defiant refusal to say what he means, excite Othello's terrified eagerness to the utmost pitch. Nothing will now satisfy him but absolute frank disclosure of "the horrible conceit." "By heaven, I 'll know thy thoughts." Then Iago insinuates that disquieting truths are best unknown, and when Othello insists, replies with a warning illustration from the torments of a jealous husband. The husband of Desdemona might well have retorted, "What is that to me? I have a wife beyond suspicion, out with your dark truth!" But Othello, instead of this, groans, "O misery!" The poison has gone home; without one overt hint he understands that Iago believes Desdemona to be false, and that is enough to bring him to the verge of believing it himself.

Having achieved this, Iago proceeds to pour on Othello's tortured mind the confirming circumstances. Othello knew them as well as he, but he had never till now attended to them or perceived their significance. Desdemona is a Venetian, and

> In Venice they do not let heaven see the pranks
> They dare not show their husbands; their best conscience
> Is not to leav 't undone, but keep 't unknown.

But Desdemona was incapable of deceit! Was he so sure of that?

<blockquote>She did deceive her father, marrying you.</blockquote>

Iago cunningly repeats the parting shaft of Brabantio as he left the Senate-house (i. 3. 294), and to Othello's obsessed mind converts the repeated warning into a prophecy perhaps already fulfilled. Iago grows more audacious as he grows more secure. He had himself declared equivocally that he thought Cassio honest (iii. 3. 125). When Othello, as if catching at the phrase, echoes it of Desdemona,

<blockquote>I do not doubt but Desdemona 's honest (ii. 3. 225),</blockquote>

Iago cries with a hardly disguised sneer,

<blockquote>Long live she so! and long live you to think so!</blockquote>

And he proceeds—with the barest apology—to make his most dangerous suggestion, that there was something unnatural in the love which Desdemona had given to the black alien, after refusing the "curled darlings" of her own clime, complexion, and degree. Othello at this point can bear no more, and abruptly dismisses him. But far from resenting his hints, or repelling them, he is sure that "this honest creature sees and knows more, far more, than he unfolds."

When they meet again (iii. 3. 330 f.) a fiercer mood has come on. He sees in Iago the cause of his torment, and torment has driven him—the least cynical of men—to adopt Iago's cynical doctrine that "'tis better to be much abused than but to know 't a little." His obsession has nevertheless suffered a check. He has seen Desdemona, and felt her hand upon his burning brow. The alternatives are not between suspicion and certainty of her guilt, but between trusting her and trusting Iago. His paralyzed judgment swings impotently to and fro—

<blockquote>I think my wife be honest, and think she is not,
I think that thou art just, and think thou art not,</blockquote>

—an intolerable state to his resolute and vehement nature, and he now for the first time calls on Iago for his evidence. Iago produces it, now no longer with feigned reluctance; that has served its purpose, and Othello, at last fully convinced, gives full rein to his passion for revenge, and vows the eternity of his hate in language of a superb and terrible beauty, which makes even his tragic infatuation sublime:

<blockquote>Never, Iago. Like to the Pontic sea, &c. (iii. 453 f.)</blockquote>

§ 11. It is needless here to dwell upon the history of Othello's mind between this point and the catastrophe. He needs no further preparation for it; even the deadly proof of her own guilt given by Desdemona in iii. 4. can add nothing to his resolve. A small man would have gone straight to its execution. Othello's will, like Hamlet's, is paralyzed by his very greatness of soul. Both have suffered the shipwreck of a faith and love possible only to a noble spirit. But the shock tells very differently on the two men. Hamlet is goaded by it to a hectic and brilliant energy; Othello, at once more passionate and less introspective, is only bewildered and confused. "Chaos comes again" with the wreck of love, as he had foretold (iii. 3. 90) before he dreamed of disaster.

It is this change which distinguishes the Othello of iv. 1. from the Othello of iii. 3. The situation is ostensibly the same. It is a second Temptation scene. Iago is reiterating his old evidence, and adding new and more monstrous proofs. Cassio has now "confessed," and Othello is made to hear him chuckle over his conquest. But Othello is no longer the man he was. His mind reels, the torturing words crowd and jostle in his brain, and he swoons. After the scene with Cassio, rage and sorrow clash together with only less incoherence:

Ay, let her rot, and perish, and be damned to-night; for she shall not live; no, my heart is turned to stone; I strike it, and it hurts my hand. O the world hath not a sweeter creature:

.   .   .   .   .

Iago. She 's the worse for all this.
Oth. O, a thousand, thousand times: and then, of so gentle a condition!
Iago. Ay, too gentle.
Oth. Nay, that 's certain: but yet the pity of it, Iago! O Iago, the pity of it, Iago! (iv. 1. 191 *f.*)

And his rage, like his sorrow, is now more violent and uncontrolled. He had swooned with grief; now, in a sudden provocation, he strikes her in public (iv. 1. 251), and, without provocation, brands her with the foulest of names. Even in the Death scene he is not secure from impulses of vindictive fury which momentarily blot out his finer mind. One such impulse cuts short his delay and ends her life; another prompts the hideous explanation to Emilia, "She 's like a liar gone to burning hell." But when this scene opens, the imminence and awfulness of the task before him have restored his self-control and quenched his anger. He is no longer the husband maddened at betrayal, but the vindicator of justice, weeping with a heavenly sorrow, and slaying what he loves, doing "nought in hate, but all in honour" (v. 2. 295). He uses the language of the world, but not altogether in the world's way. Laertes fought with Hamlet "in honour" when "satisfied in nature" (*Ham.* v. 2. 255). And Othello means his hearers to understand that he has only acted as the husband of a guilty wife was bound to act. But the force of "honour" in him is not derived from any code of gentle or military obligation. It is the persuasion of a great, passionate, veracious nature that falseness, though so lovely that the sense aches at it, must be blotted out.

§ 12. Thus wonderfully did Shakespeare create a great, tragic, and heroic figure from Cinthio's poor dupe. Only less wonderful was his transformation of the innocent victim. Desdemona, in Cinthio's tale, has hardly any definable character; she only merits her name ("the unhappy") because she chances to come to an unhappy end. But Shakespeare's persons are never thus blank or neutral; when they seem most helpless and passive, like Ophelia or Hero, they have qualities of moment for their fate. His Desdemona, then, had to have in herself one of the conditions of her "unhappy" end to co-operate innocently and unwittingly in Othello's tragedy and in her own. Cinthio had indeed given one hint of value. His Desdemona was attracted to the Moor "not by womanly passion, but by his valour." The distinction was crude; but Shakespeare, too, has made Desdemona's delight in Othello's adventures the first occasion of her passionate love,—

> She loved me for the dangers I had passed.

Her love, in other words, like his, is kindled by imagination; he is romantic, heroic, and mysterious, beyond all the men she has known; his black complexion, which Venice, in the person of its Brabantios, Iagos, and Emilias, secretly despises and derides, is for her the mark of one tanned by Arabian deserts and tropical suns. To the last something in his huge personality remains strange to her, though its fascination turns to terror, and the girl who listened rapt to his tale of monsters shudders on her deathbed at the ominous horror of his rolling eyes and convulsively contorted lips. But at the outset her admiration gives her security and confidence, she takes her fate boldly into her own hands, and astonishes, by a midnight elopement, those who only knew her as a "still and quiet" maid, who hardly moved without a blush.[1] In the Senate, too, her bearing is

---

[1] Like almost all the other heroines of Shakespeare's tragic and serious drama, it is to be noted, Desdemona has no mother. Lady

perfectly assured; she is as little overawed as Othello himself by
the authorities of the Venetian State, or by the menaces of the father
whom she has deceived. When the question is raised where she shall
stay during her husband's absence, it is she who initiates the plan
of going with him, and Othello and the Senate who comply.

Yet this girl, so clear, resolute, and self-possessed in carrying
through her union with Othello, proves utterly helpless when, a
few hours later, she has to encounter his groundless and unexplained
anger. Determined as Rosalind, nay as Helena, in compassing her
love, she suffers its frustration as unresistingly as Ophelia or Hero.
She is indeed a more exquisite character and a subtler creation than
any of these. Her lovely nature has the ardor and the innocence,
the daring and the meekness, at once, of those who know no evil.
Her father was not wrong when he spoke of her still, quiet spirit,
nor Othello when he spoke of the "gentle" Desdemona. But her
stillness and gentleness are not the signs of apathy or of well-bred
decorum; they are the seeming quiescence of a soul whose inner
ardors of passion, pity, and hero-worship have not yet been evoked.
The coming of Othello evokes them. So, in less degree, does the
engaging and chivalrous Cassio. His disgrace, like Othello's hardships, excite her pity, and without a thought of harm or of danger,
she expresses with *naïve* energy what she feels. Her eager sympathy
carries her further than the importunate pleading of iii. 3. and iii. 4.
She treats him with frank *camaraderie*, is glad when he is appointed
to Othello's command at Cyprus, and, when she thinks he is killed,
cries out "Alas, he is betrayed, and I undone!" The spirit of
enterprise which braves peril could not be more fatally united with
the *naïveté* which runs into it unawares; and the combination is not
the less deadly that both qualities spring from what is loveliest in
her nature. Her want of apprehension, in the face of Othello's
menacing demands, is not want of address, but the incapacity of
a soul utterly ignorant of evil to read the signs of it, above all, to
imagine misconstruction in the man to whom she has given her heart.
When Othello's anger at length becomes unmistakable, the shock
of the sudden dread that he does not love her shatters in a moment
all that young ardor of enterprise which his glorious apparition had
called forth. She only quails under his foul epithets, incapable even of
that momentary righteous scorn for which, in a similar situation,

---

Capulet is a mother only in name. Perdita's mother is restored to
her only at the close of the play. The unmothered loneliness or
independence of Hero, Ophelia, Cordelia, even of Rosalind, Viola,
Helena, Portia, and Perdita, is vital to their stories.

we love Imogen the more. Her unresisting self-abandonment, when the means of self-defense lay so near, might irritate us as the sign of a poor spirit, did we not hear in every word the accent of a love which no ill usage can sour or dull, and which meets death itself at his hands with no thought but to turn away the guilt from him:

> Nobody; I myself.   Farewell.
> Commend me to my kind lord, O farewell.

§ 13. The characters of Othello and Desdemona lie open before us; but something of the inscrutability which so completely masked him to the eye of his associates still clings for us to the character of "honest Iago." The villain of genius belonged to an older, more primitive type of Elizabethan hero than the noble victim of illusion. Sensational crime, deliberate and able, deeply satisfied the native taste in tragedy, as witnessed by a succession of famous creations from Appius[1] to Overreach.[2] Machiavelli was popularly believed to have provided this sensational criminal with a justifying philosophy. Shakespeare himself, always readier to touch old methods and motives to finer issues than to discard them, had in his youth been interested in the portrayal of villains of almost super-human genius, in *Titus Andronicus* and *Richard III*,—though we do not know how much of either play was of his own making. But with the deeper apprehension of tragedy which begins to appear in his work about 1600, the mere contriver of harm could no longer suffice. You shuddered at his villainies, and pitied his innocent victims; but his final ruin was simply a just Nemesis, and you left the theater cheerfully satisfied that justice had been done. Shakespeare, whether with the help of Seneca and Euripides or not, had discovered what the Greeks so profoundly understood, that the man who is the center of tragic interest must excite sympathy, however much we may condemn his acts. Macbeth touches our sympathy as Richard never does. In the earliest of the mature tragedies even the men who entangle the hero in his tragic errors excite pity at moments. Our scorn for Claudius relaxes in his prayer; and Cassius, despite his base motives for slaying Cæsar, is more pathetic than Brutus himself. But the completely unsympathetic criminal, in this secondary capacity, was never excluded; if *King Lear* beyond all the other tragedies resembles a giant conflict between good and evil, it is because an Edmund, a Goneril, and a Regan contrive the harms; while the villain Iachimo, in the less somber tragedy of *Cymbeline*,

---

[1] *Appius and Virginia*, c. 1563.
[2] *A New Way to Pay Old Debts*, by Massinger, c. 1625.

is, no more than Edmund, saved from our loathing by his late repentance. Earlier than all these, and superior to them all in profundity of conception and wealth of psychological detail, is the Iago of our play.

Hazlitt declared Iago to be "one of Shakespeare's works of supererogation." Certainly, for effecting the tragic business of the play, a far simpler and more ordinary rogue would have served. Othello's happiness could have been wrecked by a being imagined with less daring originality. But economy of power was not much in Shakespeare's way. His bent, in characterization as in style, is towards a glorious excess, disproportioned to, or even, as in Shylock and Falstaff, in conflict with, the primary purpose of the play. There is no such conflict here. Iago never touches our sympathies for a moment; Othello from beginning to end excites our warmest love and pity. But in intellectual and dramatic interest Iago's rôle fully equals Othello's, and the ambitious tragic actor chooses it as often.

For Iago, unlike the Shakespearean criminals who most resemble him, offers a problem. Edmund and Richard are simply ambitious and unscrupulous men who want a duchy or a kingdom, and plot the death of father or nephews to get it. We do not ask why they plot thus, for their action is a commonplace of history. But Iago's case resists these facile explanations. It is not merely that his plot is a peculiarly horrible outrage, or that his alleged grounds for it are utterly disproportionate, or that his reputation in astute and censorious Venice for honesty is hard to reconcile with his consummate virtuosity in crime. All this is true. But Shakespeare did not mean Iago to be an ordinary rogue. He was not, in particular, to be like his original, a rejected lover who avenges himself by slandering the lady to her husband. This stock personage of Italian romance did not in the least interest Shakespeare.[1] The revenge motive, so popular at this time on the stage, was now not good enough for him; and we see in Iago, as in Hamlet, how he transformed it. Iago does not love Desdemona, being incapable of loving anyone. He inclines to think that Cassio loves her (ii. 1. 296), and even that she loves him, but these facts only interest him as points favoring the success of his game. Several other motives are, however, suggested by Iago himself, and though his evidence is never to be implicitly trusted, it cannot be ignored.

We learn, at the outset, that he "hates" Othello for having made Cassio lieutenant instead of himself (i. 1. 6 f.). Later (i. 3. 393,

---

[1] He made a similar change in the parallel case of *Much Ado*. Don John, like Iago, has no grudge against the lady, only a dispassionate taste for wrecking marriages.

ii. 1. 304 *f.*) it appears that he suspects Othello of having seduced his wife, and, later still, that he likewise suspects Cassio (ii. 1. 316). But Iago is not the kind of man whom offences like these goad into action. He is too profoundly immoral to feel the sting of wounded honor, and too conscious of his power to be gravely concerned about office and rank. He is exempt from most of the mortifications which torment weaker and better men. The basis of his character is a union of absolute egoism with prodigious intellectual force. His passionless cynicism is hardly more capable of hate than it is of love. When he says he "loves" Desdemona (ii. 1. 300), he means merely that he proposes to be "evened with" Othello "wife for wife" for his supposed seduction of Emilia. When he says he "hates" Othello (*ib.*), he means that he has various plausible reasons for hating him, and intends to act as if these were driving him on. He frankly appreciates the fine qualities of his intended victims. Cassio has "a daily beauty in his life which makes me ugly"; Othello ("howbeit I endure him not") "is of a constant, loving, noble nature." Nor does he in the least palliate the vileness of his own course. His plot is a "monstrous birth" which "hell and night" are needed to bring forth (i. 3. 409). And he compares his plausible management of it to the cunning of devils, who when they will

> the blackest sins put on
> They do suggest at first with heavenly shows. (ii. 3. 356.)

But this is a purely intellectual recognition of moral values, wholly untouched by moral emotion. Iago is a master of the ways of men, as Othello sees, and reads character, as far as his perverted instincts permit, with extreme penetration, but without either desire or regret. His moral indifference passes for good nature, as his craft passes for wisdom, and his cynicism for the sincerity of a "heart that passion cannot rule" (iii. 3. 123). He has the heart and brain of Goethe's Mephistopheles, but disguises it even better than he; Milton's Satan, who has tears "such as angels weep," and feels a pang of anguish at the sight of Adam and Eve "imparadised in one another's arms," is far less diabolic than Iago.

Like Mephistopheles, too (and like Richard, but unlike Satan), Iago has humor—the ironic humor of a strong man easily secure in his strength, who can afford to play with his victims; the cynical humor which reduces everything to the lowest terms, and caps a compliment with an anticlimax. His dialogue with Desdemona and Emilia, after their landing at Cyprus, is genial, even gay in tone, but his sardonic temper and gross fancy constantly break through:

and his description of "a deserving woman indeed," and what she is good for, leads up only to that "most lame and impotent conclusion," as even the gentle Desdemona calls it, that she is "to suckle fools and chronicle small beer."

Iago is here at his ease, in undress, as it were, and as much himself as he ever appears when not alone. The serious business of the plot has not yet begun, is not even completely shaped in his mind; and in the meantime he is ready to amuse his general's lady with brilliant sword-play of wit. Not that he cares a jot for the aching anxiety she is trying to beguile. He even lets himself go with a cynical brutality which belongs to his character, not to the part, provoking Desdemona's final comment, "What say you, Cassio? Is he not a most profane and liberal [*licentious*] counsellor?" and Cassio's chivalrous apology for him as a blunt soldier, accustomed to "speak home."

But in general we see Iago playing a part for a definite end, and with consummate skill. He is so inveterate and so masterly an actor that all the world calls him "honest Iago." To the poor dupe Roderigo he expounds himself at the outset with contemptuous unreserve:

> In following [the Moor] I follow but myself;
> Heaven is my judge, not I for love and duty,
> But seeming so, for my peculiar end;
> For when my outward action doth demonstrate
> The native act and figure of my heart
> In compliment extern, 't is not long after
> But I will wear my heart upon my sleeve
> For daws to peck at: I am not what I am. (i. 1. 58 *f.*).

His virtuosity in this art is seen when he has to play a part that seems in conflict with his saturnine and passionless nature, as when he leads the revel in song and jest in the drinking-scene (iii. 3), or caps the glowing poetry of Othello's vow with a very fair counterfeit (iii. 3. 463 *f.*); while the tragic catastrophe itself attests the power he throws into his impersonation of the honest friend who reluctantly opens the eyes of a deluded husband. And Iago is not without the actor's zest in his own play. But it never for a moment beguiles him to forget his situation and his purpose. "Art for art" has no attraction for this artist. Every stroke and gesture is profoundly calculated, but for an end outside the play.[1] He is, as Hazlitt said, "an amateur of tragedy in real life." He arranges

---

[1] As in *Hamlet* and—less notably—*Macbeth*, Shakespeare presents this important character in part by means of a series of soliloquies. For the Elizabethans, the soliloquy was a dramatic convention

a drama, and acts the leading part; but the blood must be real blood, and the death real death. His sport is the play of a prodigiously active intellect in the service of a lawless will. And the force that at bottom impels him beyond whatever ends of ambition or revenge he professes to pursue is the masterful egoist's "will to power." His plot satisfies this instinct in two ways. It is spun finely from the cunning substance of his own brain. And it works swift and dramatic ruin in the lives of fortunate men. Evil is Iago's good. The base hint of mischief afoot fires his imagination. At the very outset the idea of vexing Othello's new joy releases the springs of his invention,—

> Poison his delight,
> Proclaim him in the streets; incense her kinsmen.
> And, though he in a fertile climate dwell,
> Plague him with flies, . . .

—that same invention which, when invited to praise a good and beautiful woman, comes from his brain "as birdlime does from frize," the hard birth of a laboring muse:

> Put me not to it, gentle lady,
> For I am nothing if not critical.

§ 14. Iago's wife, Emilia, is a commonplace, worldly, rather sensual woman, sullenly submissive to her husband, immeasurably below him in intellect, and not obviously above him in character. She fills through the greater part of the play an unattractive, even ignoble rôle. She wonders that any wife should refuse to be false to her marriage vows for a sufficient consideration, and in her own case we surmise that the consideration need not be very large (iv. 3). If we reject Iago's suspicion that she has been the mistress of Othello or of Cassio, it is not because we think her incapable of it. In the matter of the handkerchief she lends herself, stupidly but innocently, to Iago's purpose, which she might have known could not possibly bode good. When Othello calls for it, and Desdemona is in distress for its loss, Emilia, who could have explained the matter in a moment, remains silent, in dread of her husband. This is a

which permitted the dramatist on occasion to show what was going on in the speaker's *mind:*—it matters little whether it is thought of as uttered audibly. The student will find it worth while to give particular attention to this remarkable series of Iago's soliloquies: i. 3. 389–410; ii. 1. 294–321; ii. 3. 50–65; ii. 3. 342–368; ii. 3. 388–394; iii. 3. 321–333; iv. 1. 45–58; iv. 1. 101–104; v. 1. 11–22; v. 1. 128–129.

gross lapse, but there is no ground for suspecting that she is aware of his plot and deliberately plays into his hands. Her amazed iteration when she learns the truth ("My husband!" v. 2. 140 f.) makes that clear. Desdemona has deeply touched her shallow, mundane heart. A woman so "heavenly pure" had never come within her ken before. Even in the case of the lost handkerchief she gives way unwillingly, and pleads feebly to have it returned to "the poor lady," who will "run mad when she shall lack it." But when she hears (for she has been listening at the door) Othello in the inner chamber lay the foulest terms upon his wife, her anger breaks out fiercely against the slanderer who has abused the Moor (iv. 2. 130 f.). And when she sees Desdemona dead, and by Othello's hand, she flames into a passion of indignant grief which overpowers all thought of her own safety, or of respect for her husband's chief, as, a few minutes later, it overpowers her more genuine awe of her husband himself. In vain Iago, checkmated by the unforeseen move of this despised pawn, threatens her, and she scorns to be silent now:

> I peace?
> No, I will speak as liberal as the north:
> Let heaven and men and devils, let them all,
> All, all, cry shame against me, yet I 'll speak!

And so, echoing with her last breath her mistress's willow-song, she "dies in music."

§ 15. Like Emilia, Roderigo is Iago's tool; like her, he dies by Iago's hand; like her, he contributes something (though far less) to the ultimate exposure. Shakespeare has created few more contemptible persons. His pretensions to Desdemona's hand have been cut short by his formal exclusion from her house. When she is married to Othello he has thoughts of drowning himself, but is easily cajoled to exchange his money and jewels for the possession of her person.

§ 16. Brabantio is of concern to the plot, both as the father of Desdemona and as a typical Venetian senator. His love for his daughter was deep—for her loss killed him—but it was imperious and without understanding, like Lear's. We pity him in the opening scene, unnerved with anguish and anxiety at the first news of Desdemona's flight. But he is utterly incapable of understanding her love for Othello, whom he himself has "loved" and listened to with delight, and his peremptory rejection of her when she claims leave to prefer her husband to her father,

> God be wi' you, I have done,
> Please it your grace, on to the state affairs,

is as revolting, in its kind, as the corresponding outburst of the father of Cordelia. But a father thus fiercely jealous of his paternal rights was required by the plot, and the final reason of his dramatic existence is perhaps disclosed in the parting shot, afterwards used with such deadly effect, as already noted, by Iago:

> She has deceived her father, and may thee.

But Brabantio is also a great Venetian magnifico. He is "beloved" (i. 2. 12) and influential, with powerful friends, whose support he can command at need (i. 1. 181). In council his voice counts with the Doge's, and he can bandy proverbs with that dignitary on equal terms. His relations with Othello symbolize those of the State. He entertains the black alien as an amusing visitor, and indignantly spurns him when he presumes to win the daughter of the house. The republic, too, shows astute compliance towards the invaluable soldier when the Turk threatens, and promptly cashiers him (doubtless at Brabantio's urgency) when the danger is past.

Brabantio's brother, Gratiano, and his kinsman Lodovico, are slightly touched. Gratiano tells us of Brabantio's death (v. 2. 204 f.), and thinks him happy to have died. He is an elderly Venetian, and though we must beware of seeking too much meaning in a few brief speeches, we surmise in him something of the unmilitary disposition natural both to old age and to a community which carried on its wars by deputy. He stands armed to guard Othello's chamber, but starts back in dismay when he sees that Othello, too, is armed (v. 2. 269). And when Othello has stabbed himself, his shocked exclamation, "All that 's spoke is marr'd," completely inverts the feeling of the modern spectator that this end was as right as it was inevitable.

Lodovico, a younger man, is a good example of the Venetian envoy or "civil servant," well-bred and courteous, but with energetic speech and action at command. When Othello strikes his wife in his presence, his protest goes to the utmost of what was possible, within the forms of good breeding, towards an offender in Othello's authoritative position.

The Duke and the Senator represent, in the Council scene, the astute "State" of Venice, as conceived in Elizabethan England. The situation with which they are confronted makes an unusual demand upon their statecraft, but they are equal to it. One suspects that every senator, including the Duke—despite his comment on Othello's tale—would have acted like Brabantio had his own daughter been in question. Before the culprit is identified, the utmost severity of the law is promised to the vindictive father. But when he proves to be the indispensable general, the tone of the Court undergoes a marked though tacit change. The Duke now takes the lead in smoothing away the offence, and calls in his suavest platitudes to placate Brabantio, drawing on himself the merited irony of his retort. But the public business is urgent, the private quarrel is glossed over, the old father withdraws—to die of grief—while the famous general of the State is sent off post-hate to repel the national peril and succumb to the deadlier peril which awaits himself.

Montano, Othello's predecessor in the governorship of Cyprus, but still young, has served under him, and, like Cassio, admires and honors him. "The man commands like a full soldier" (ii. 1. 35). He is glad of Othello's appointment, and as anxious as Cassio for his safety in the storm. But he has nothing of Cassio's mercurial ardor. Venice ascribes to him a "gravity and stillness" rare at his years, while sagacious elders prize his wisdom. Cassio's failing, in an officer so highly placed, revolts his sense of political propriety even more than his sense of decorum. He joins in the drinking bout at some little risk to his high reputation, but is the first to call his comrades to their military duties, and he incurs his wound in trying to stop the fray. Othello, finding Cassio incapable of explaining matters, turns at once to Montano, as the man from whom the whole truth and nothing but the truth was most likely to be had, astonishing as it was to find him there:

Worthy Montano, you were wont to be civil.

Even honest Iago might be too indulgent to a fellow-officer!

Bianca, Cassio's mistress, replaces two persons in Cinthio's tale—his wife, who is seen at her window copying the embroidery in Disdemona's handkerchief, and the courtesan to whom he is on his way when attacked by Iago. Shakespeare never introduces characters of this type except with a definite technical purpose in view, and the immense superiority of the drama at this point is beyond question. Cassio does not (like the Captain) recognize the handkerchief as Desdemona's. He cannot therefore try to return it, and quite naturally gives it to Bianca to be copied; while she, angrily suspecting it to be the gift of "some minx," returns it to him precisely at the moment when Othello and Iago are looking on (iv. 3. 151 f.). And Bianca was far more likely than his wife to provoke Cassio to those fleers and gibes and notable scorns (iv. 1. 83) which Othello is to interpret as the signs of his triumph over Desdemona. For the rest, this courtesan is raised above the grossness of her occupation by her love for Cassio, egoistic, jealous, and vindictive as it is.

Were it not that an official jester was usually attached to the staff of great Elizabethan houses, and is thus not out of place in the household of the general of Venice, the Clown of this play might be described as the most perfunctory personage in the entire Shakespearean drama. It was a convention of the Elizabethan stage that there should be at least one low-comedy part in each play, no matter how serious; and Shakespeare, following the usual custom, in his maturer plays commonly gave this clownish character some real dramatic significance, as with the grave-digger in *Hamlet* and the Fool in *Lear*. But in *Othello* he does not seem to have been in the mood to make the Clown scenes anything but pure interludes, and they are very often omitted in presentations of the play.

§ 17. An attempt has been made in the foregoing paragraphs to sketch the lines of the transformation which Cinthio's tale underwent in the mind of Shakespeare. How was the great tragedy which resulted related to the other examples of his mature tragic art? In one point, the character of the hero, the question has been answered already (§ 7). But while Shakespeare's tragic heroes have certain constant traits, and, with all their wonderful diversity, can be grouped, his tragic plots, with all their individual excellence, seem to defy classification; and it remains to ask, finally, how the plot of *Othello* is related, as plot, to the rest.

In several of the tragedies the conflict—inner or outer—has a succession of phases. The hero and his party first triumph over all obstacles: Macbeth is crowned, Cæsar slain, Claudius is convicted of the murder. Then the opposing forces rally, and finally prevail. In these plays there is a culminating moment, usually in the third act, sometimes surpassing in interest the catastrophe at the close of the fifth, while the interval between these is usually of less absorbing power (cf. the fourth act of *Macbeth*, *Hamlet*, *Julius Cæsar*, *King Lear*, with the third and fifth).[1] In *Othello* the structure is totally different. The tragic action proper begins only with the second act, and goes on with continuous and gathering intensity to the end. It is as if Macbeth first conceived his plot against Duncan at the close of the first act, and compassed his end by a protracted intrigue through the remainder of the play, to perish himself with his victim at the end. Instead of an action with two moments of

---

[1] On the devices by which Shakespeare meets the defects of this type of plot, cf. Bradley, *Shakespearean Tragedy*, p. 55 *f.*

nearly equal intensity, we have a main action ascending continuously to a final climax, preceded by a preparatory first act. There is nothing like this elsewhere in Shakespeare.

Moreover, this main action of *Othello* is distinguished among Shakespeare's plots by its simplicity and directness. It is his nearest approach to the "classical" severity of Sophocles and Racine. Hence, in part, its early popularity in France. *Macbeth* comes nearest in simplicity, but its course is not equally direct and continuous. It stands in still sharper contrast here with *Hamlet*, which preceded, and with *Lear*, which followed. In *Hamlet* and *Lear* Shakespeare resorts, for instance, with extraordinary effect, to those repetitions of the theme in another key which add so much to the charm of his comedies. Laertes's demeanor as the son of a murdered father serves as a burlesque foil to the tragic inaction of Hamlet. Gloucester's bodily torment at the hands of an ungrateful son accentuates the mental agony of Lear. There is nothing of this in the action proper of our play. From the landing in Cyprus onward, no other interest is allowed to conflict even remotely with the absorbing dread, indignation, and suspense excited by Iago's game. Cassio's dismissal moves our sympathy, but pity gives way to an acute anxiety when we realize that Desdemona's pleading for his reinstatement is to be the web which will fatally ensnare them both. Bianca and Roderigo count only as tools of Iago, and have no other value in the play. Even the public and military interest, promised at the outset by the menace of the Turkish attack, is promptly eliminated when its purpose has been served, and the agents and victims of the tragedy have been assembled at its scene in Cyprus. Even the desperate tempest, though vividly touched, is of value chiefly because, by disabling the Turkish fleet, it enables the Venetian general to come to the port where Desdemona and Iago await him.

But the first act has a quite different character. Not only are several distinct actions opened, any one of which might conceivably prove to be the dominant motive of the play, but the motive which is actually to dominate it is not announced, or even imagined, till the very close. Othello's secret marriage, Brabantio's vindictive passion, and his favor for the rejected Roderigo, seem to foreshadow a drama of intrigue between rival lovers. The Turkish menace and the post-haste dispatch of Othello suggest a drama in which, as in *Julius Cæsar*, the fortunes of the State are dramatically no less momentous than the fate of a man, while Iago, the real and sole initiator of the action which is to blot out all the rest, appears still a secondary figure, his formidable animosities already vaguely stirring, but not yet projected into any determined scheme of action. The first act has thus almost the air of a little independent drama— a drama with an ironically happy ending; for the triumph of Othello in vindicating his marriage, and that of Desdemona in being allowed to accompany him, create the conditions which seal their doom.

If this were a complete statement of the relation between the first act and the sequel, the play would be liable to the damaging charge of falling into two parts rather loosely connected. But, in fact, every line of the first act has its function in the economy of the entire drama. Everything in it serves either (1) to bring about the conditions from which the tragic action is to spring, or (2) to make its course irresistible and its issue inevitable. To this second purpose some of Shakespeare's finest psychological artistry is devoted. Othello's account of his courtship effectually vindicates his marriage; but it also enables us to understand how such a union could be destroyed. His instant—nay joyous—response to the call of honorable duty, an hour after his marriage, foretells the husband who will later sacrifice his wife, doing "nought in hate, but all in honour." Desdemona's innocent boldness, in the courtship, in her defense of her love, and in her appeal to go to the campaign with Othello, prepares us for her dangerous importunity in demanding the reinstatement of Cassio. Roderigo, the fatuous discarded suitor, pursuing the runaway bride under Iago's astute direction, is already the compliant tool who will provoke Cassio in the drunken brawl or undertake to put him out of the way. And if Iago himself only at the close conceives his plot, the sinister power and absolute egoism of the man oppress the atmosphere from his very opening words; we know from the first that there is no design, however destructive, from which he will shrink, and no weapon, however deadly, that he will hesitate to use. The picture, finally, of the society and government of Venice, and of the position of Othello, at once flattering and insecure in relation to both, provides a setting and atmosphere to which this story of astute calculation, romantic attraction, and tragic misunderstanding is entirely congenial.

While *Othello* thus satisfies with extraordinary completeness the "classical" demand for structural unity and coherence, it does this in a way entirely true to the genius of Elizabethan dramatic art. If it is wanting in some favorite tragic motives—battles, madness, ghosts, spectacles, revenge—it has many other, often unobtrusive, links with the native stage. The sharp detachment of the first act in place and in time, the infusion of grim comedy, the foolery of the Clown, the murders on the stage, the catholicity of poetic range, from the acrid obscenities of Iago to the oriental splendor and sibylline strangeness of Othello's imagination—in all this it is racy of the soil. The well-known story of the resentment roused in the first French audience that witnessed it [1] by the introduction of a *mouchoir* into tragedy symbolizes the amplitude of Shakespearean art, taking in at once the highest and the homeliest things, of which it is perhaps the supreme example.

§ 18. What, finally, does *Othello* contribute to our impression of the mind of Shakespeare? A daring question, but the critical interpreter must not decline it. We can at least put aside some mistaken conclusions about the poet, derived from mistaken ideas about the play—the idea of "poetic justice," for instance. A certain class of critics and readers insist on discovering a quasi-justification for Desdemona's tragedy. She is a warning against filial disobedience, or against marrying a member of another race. These trivialities have been seriously entertained.[2] The notion which underlies them is two-fold: (1) That the play represents a world dominated by a moral order, and (2) that this moral order asserts itself by satisfactions and sufferings proportional to good and evil conduct. The second is glaringly contradicted by the facts of the Shakespearean drama. In our play—putting Desdemona apart—who will measure the agony of Othello by the unwitting wrong he does—not in hate, but "all in honour"? The first is true within limits. Good and evil are not indifferent in the Shakespearean drama. Evil is a disturbing and anarchic element, and it finally perishes. The doom which overtakes his contrivers of harm has the air of reasserting the moral law they transgress. But we must not speak of any relation between suffering and wrongdoing. Innocence and goodness are crushed with evil; the result of the "overthrow of evil" may be a grievous destruction of good. Even the men who have brought on the calamities in which they perish may, by perishing, impoverish the capacity of the world for good. Not merely Hamlet and Lear, but Macbeth and Antony, leave behind them a society guided by men who may be free from their weakness but are without their towering strength and their appeal to something deeper and more potent in ourselves. In *Othello* this waste of goodness is as extreme as is the power and daring of evil. Iago may be handed over to unimaginable tortures, but the total result is a hideous and horrible triumph of evil under

---

[1] At the performance of de Vigny's version, October 24, 1829. The first performance, in 1792, did not offer this incident, the translator, Ducis, prudently substituting an intercepted letter for the offensive handkerchief.

[2] See Furness's New Variorum edition, pp. 422–28, 445.

an all-deceiving "honest" mask. Did Shakespeare feel in these facts the problem that perplexes the theological or philosophic idealist? Perhaps; but at least he never suggests its solution. Christian or theistic ideas, though occasionally alluded to, never have any part in the economy of the action or in coloring its issues. It is never hinted that this world, with its clashing discords, is a member of a larger whole where partial evil will prove to be universal good. As little does he suggest that the master force in these tragic calamities is a blind or malignant fate thrusting men to their doom. Yet, on the other hand, the intensity of ethical feeling which has gone to the creation of the harrowing conflicts of the great tragedies, most of all, perhaps, in our play, forbids us to think of him as lightly accepting, with the prosperous man's shrug of the shoulders, a world in which Iagos are produced and Desdemonas strangled, in which, for the rest, lawsuits were successful, and the Stratford tithes regularly paid. The creator of Shakespearean tragedy was in no danger of making light of the enormous power of men for mischief. But he saw, too, with unparalleled clearness, how this huge complex manifold nature of things, which produces Iagos and Gonerils, produces also Desdemonas and Cordelias, whose ineffable beauty of goodness shines out most clearly in and through their calamities; that their tragic doom does not lessen the worth for humanity of their having been; and that the human seed and soil in which such flowers bud and burgeon cannot be wholly void of the grounds of faith and hope.

OTHELLO

THE MOOR OF VENICE

DRAMATIS PERSONÆ

DUKE OF VENICE.
BRABANTIO, a Senator.
Other Senators.
GRATIANO, brother to Brabantio.
LODOVICO, kinsman to Brabantio.
OTHELLO, a noble Moor in the service of the Venetian State.
CASSIO, his lieutenant.
IAGO, his ancient.
RODERIGO, a Venetian gentleman.
MONTANO, Othello's predecessor in the government of Cyprus.
Clown, servant to Othello.

DESDEMONA, daughter to Brabantio and wife to Othello.
EMILIA, wife to Iago.
BIANCA, mistress to Cassio.

Sailor, Messenger, Herald, Officers, Gentlemen, Musicians and Attendants.

SCENE—The first act in Venice; during the rest of the play, at seaport in Cyprus.

———————

Historic Period: May, 1570

OTHELLO

THE MOOR OF VENICE

ACT I

SCENE I — *Venice.   A street*

Enter RODERIGO *and* IAGO

Rod.   Tush! never tell me; I take it much unkindly
That thou, Iago, who hast had my purse
As if the strings were thine, shouldst know of this.

Iago.   'Sblood, but you will not hear me:
If ever I did dream of such a matter
Abhor me.

Rod.   Thou told'st me thou didst hold him in thy
  hate.

Iago.   Despise me, if I do not.   Three great ones
  of the city,
In personal suit to make me his lieutenant,
Off-capp'd to him: and, by the faith of man,   10
I know my price, I am worth no worse a place:
But he, as loving his own pride and purposes,
Evades them, with a bombast circumstance
Horribly stuff'd with epithets of war;
And, in conclusion,
Nonsuits my mediators: for, "Certes," says he,
"I have already chose my officer."
And what was he?
Forsooth, a great arithmetician,

1

One Michael Cassio, a Florentine,   20
A fellow almost damn'd in a fair wife;
That never set a squadron in the field,
Nor the division of a battle knows
More than a spinster; unless the bookish theoric,
Wherein the toged consuls can propose
As masterly as he: mere prattle, without practice,
In all his soldiership. But he, sir, had the election:
And I, of whom his eyes had seen the proof
At Rhodes, at Cyprus and on other grounds
Christian and heathen, must be be-lee'd and calm'd   30
By debitor and creditor: this counter-caster,
He, in good time, must his lieutenant be,
And I — God bless the mark! — his Moorship's
          ancient.
   Rod.   By heaven, I rather would have been his
          hangman.
   Iago.   Why, there 's no remedy; 't is the curse
          of service,
Preferment goes by letter and affection,
And not by old gradation, where each second
Stood heir to the first. Now, sir, be judge yourself,
Whether I in any just term am affined
To love the Moor.
   Rod.   I would not follow him then.   40
   Iago.   O, sir, content you;
I follow him to serve my turn upon him:
We cannot all be masters, nor all masters
Cannot be truly follow'd. You shall mark
Many a duteous and knee-crooking knave,
That, doting on his own obsequious bondage,
Wears out his time, much like his master's ass,

For nought but provender, and when he 's old,
      cashier'd:
Whip me such honest knaves.   Others there are
Who, trimm'd in forms and visages of duty,   50
Keep yet their hearts attending on themselves,
And, throwing but shows of service on their lords,
Do well thrive by them, and when they have lined
      their coats
Do themselves homage: these fellows have some
      soul;
And such a one do I profess myself.   For, sir,
It is as sure as you are Roderigo,
Were I the Moor, I would not be Iago:
In following him, I follow but myself;
Heaven is my judge, not I for love and duty,
But seeming so, for my peculiar end: 60
For when my outward action doth demonstrate
The native act and figure of my heart
In compliment extern, 't is not long after
But I will wear my heart upon my sleeve
For daws to peck at: I am not what I am.
    Rod.   What a full fortune does the thick-lips owe,
If he carry 't thus!
    Iago.   Call up her father,
Rouse him: make after him, poison his delight,
Proclaim him in the streets; incense her kinsmen,
And, though he in a fertile climate dwell,   70
Plague him with flies: though that his joy be joy,
Yet throw such changes of vexation on 't,
As it may lose some colour.
    Rod.   Here is her father's house; I 'll call aloud.
    Iago.   Do; with like timorous accent and dire yell

As when, by night and negligence, the fire
Is spied in populous cities.

    Rod.   What, ho, Brabantio! Signior Brabantio,
        ho!

    Iago.   Awake! what, ho, Brabantio! thieves!
        thieves! thieves!

Look to your house, your daughter and your bags!   80
Thieves! thieves!

Brabantio appears above, at a window

    Bra.   What is the reason of this terrible summons?
What is the matter there?

    Rod.   Signior, is all your family within?

    Iago.   Are your doors lock'd?

    Bra.   Why, wherefore ask you this?

    Iago.   'Zounds, sir, you 're robb'd; for shame, put
        on your gown;

Your heart is burst, you have lost half your soul;
Even now, now, very now, arise, arise;
Awake the snorting citizens with the bell,   90
Or else the devil will make a grandsire of you:
Arise, I say.

    Bra.   What, have you lost your wits?

    Rod.   Most reverend signior, do you know my
        voice?

    Bra.   Not I: what are you?

    Rod.   My name is Roderigo.

    Bra.   The worser welcome:
I have charged thee not to haunt about my doors:
In honest plainness thou hast heard me say
My daughter is not for thee; and now, in madness,
Being full of supper and distempering draughts,

Upon malicious bravery, dost thou come   100
To start my quiet.

   Rod. Sir, sir, sir,—

   Bra.   But thou must needs be sure
My spirit and my place have in them power
To make this bitter to thee.

   Rod.   Patience, good sir.

   Bra. What tell'st thou me of robbing? this is
        Venice;
My house is not a grange.

   Rod.   Most grave Brabantio,
In simple and pure soul I come to you.

   Iago. 'Zounds, sir, you are one of those that will
not serve God, if the devil bid you. Because we
come to do you service and you think we are ruffians,
you 'll have your daughter covered with a Barbary
horse; you' ll have your nephews neigh to you;
you 'll have coursers for cousins and gennets for
germans.

   Bra. Thou art a villain.

   Iago.   You are — a senator.   11ᴢ

   Bra. This thou shalt answer; I know thee, Rod-
        erigo.

   Rod. Sir, I will answer any thing. But, I be-
        seech you,
If 't be your pleasure and most wise consent,
As partly I find it is, that your fair daughter,
At this odd-even and dull watch o' the night,
Transported, with no worse nor better guard
But with a knave of common hire, a góndolier,
To the gross clasps of a lascivious Moor, —
If this be known to you and your allowance,

We then have done you bold and saucy wrongs;
But if you know not this, my manners tell me   130
We have your wrong rebuke.   Do not believe
That, from the sense of all civility,
I thus would play and trifle with your reverence:
Your daughter, if you have not given her leave,
I say again, hath made a gross revolt;
Tying her duty, beauty, wit and fortunes
In an extravagant and wheeling stranger
Of here and every where. Straight satisfy yourself:
If she be in her chamber or your house,
Let loose on me the justice of the state   140
For thus deluding you.

   Bra.   Strike on the tinder, ho!
Give me a taper! call up all my people!
This accident is not unlike my dream:
Belief of it oppresses me already.
Light, I say! light!   *[Exit above.*

   Iago.   Farewell; for I must leave you:
It seems not meet, nor wholesome to my place,
To be produced — as, if I stay, I shall —
Against the Moor: for, I do know, the state,
However this may gall him with some check,
Cannot with safety cast him, for he 's embark'd   150
With such loud reason to the Cyprus wars,
Which even now stand in act, that, for their
       souls,
Another of his fathom they have none,
To lead their business: in which regard,
Though I do hate him as I do hell-pains,
Yet for necessity of present life,
I must show out a flag and sign of love,

Which is indeed but sign. That you shall surely
    find him,
Lead to the Sagittary the raised search;   159
And there will I be with him. So farewell.   [*Exit.*

Enter, below, Brabantio, *in his night-gown,*
and Servants *with torches*

  Bra.   It is too true an evil: gone she is;
And what 's to come of my despised time
Is nought but bitterness. Now, Roderigo,
Where didst thou see her?   O unhappy girl!
With the Moor, say'st thou? Who would be a father!
How didst thou know 't was she? O, she deceives me
Past thought! What said she to you? Get more
    tapers;
Raise all my kindred. Are they married, think you?
  Rod.   Truly, I think they are.
  Bra.   O heaven! How got she out? O treason of
    the blood!   170
Fathers, from hence trust not your daughters' minds
By what you see them act. Is there not charms
By which the property of youth and maidhood
May be abused? Have you not read, Roderigo,
Of some such thing?
  Rod.   Yes, sir, I have indeed.
  Bra.   Call up my brother. O, would you had
    had her!
Some one way, some another. Do you know
Where we may apprehend her and the Moor?
  Rod.   I think I can discover him, if you please
To get good guard and go along with me.   180
  Bra.   Pray you, lead on. At every house I 'll call;

I may command at most.   Get weapons, ho!
And raise some special officers of night.
On, good Roderigo: I 'll deserve your pains.   [*Exeunt.*

SCENE II — *Another street*
Enter OTHELLO, IAGO, *and* Attendants *with torches*

Iago.   Though in the trade of war I have slain
          men,
Yet do I hold it very stuff o' the conscience
To do no cóntrived murder: I lack iniquity
Sometimes to do me service: nine or ten times
I had thought to have yerk'd him here under the ribs.
   Oth.   'T is better as it is.
   Iago.   Nay, but he prated,
And spoke such scurvy and provoking terms
Against your honour
That, with the little godliness I have,
I did full hard forbear him.   But, I pray you, sir,   10
Are you fast married?   Be assured of this,
That the magnifico is much beloved,
And hath in his effect a voice potential
As double as the duke's: he will divorce you,
Or put upon you what restraint and grievance
The law, with all his might to enforce it on,
Will give him cable.
   Oth.   Let him do his spite:
My services which I have done the signiory
Shall out-tongue his complaints.   'T is yet to know,—
Which, when I know that boasting is an honour,   20
I shall promulgate — I fetch my life and being
From men of royal siege, and my demerits

May speak unbonneted to as proud a fortune
As this that I have reach'd: for know, Iago,
But that I love the gentle Desdemona,
I would not my unhoused free condition
Put into circumscription and confine
For the sea's worth.   But, look! what lights come
       yond?

  Iago.   Those are the raised father and his friends:
You were best go in.

  Oth.   Not I: I must be found: 30
My parts, my title and my perfect soul
Shall manifest me rightly.   Is it they?

  Iago.   By Janus, I think no.

     Enter CASSIO, *and certain* Officers *with torches*

  Oth.   The servants of the duke, and my lieutenant.
The goodness of the night upon you, friends!
What is the news?

  Cas.   The duke does greet you, general,
And he requires your haste-post-haste appearance,
Even on the instant.

  Oth.   What is the matter, think you?

  Cas.   Something from Cyprus, as I may divine:
It is a business of some heat: the galleys   40
Have sent a dozen sequent messengers
This very night at one another's heels,
And many of the consuls, raised and met,
Are at the duke's already: you have been hotly
       call'd for;
When, being not at your lodging to be found,
The senate hath sent about three several quests
To search you out.

Oth.   'T is well I am found by you.
I will but spend a word here in the house,
And go with you.   [*Exit.*
    Cas.   Ancient, what makes he here?
    Iago.   'Faith, he to-night hath boarded a land
        carack:
If it prove lawful prize, he 's made for ever.   51
    Cas.   I do not understand.
    Iago.   He 's married.
    Cas.   To who?

Re-enter OTHELLO

    Iago.   Marry, to — Come, captain, will you go?
    Oth.   Have with you.
    Cas.   Here comes another troop to seek for you.
    Iago.   It is Brabantio.   General, be advised;
He comes to bad intent.

Enter BRABANTIO, RODERIGO, *and* Officers *with torches and weapons*

    Oth.   Holla! stand there!
    Rod.   Signior, it is the Moor.
    Bra.   Down with him, thief!
                    [*They draw on both sides.*
    Iago.   You, Roderigo! come, sir, I am for you.
    Oth.   Keep up your bright swords, for the dew
        will rust them.
Good signior, you shall more command with years   60
Than with your weapons.
    Bra.   O thou foul thief, where hast thou stow'd
        my daughter?

Damn'd as thou art, thou hast enchanted her;
For I 'll refer me to all things of sense,
If she in chains of magic were not bound,
Whether a maid so tender, fair and happy,
So opposite to marriage that she shunn'd
The wealthy curled darlings of our nation,
Would ever have, to incur a general mock,
Run from her guardage to the sooty bosom   70
Of such a thing as thou, to fear, not to delight.
Judge me the world, if 't is not gross in sense
That thou hast practised on her with foul charms,
Abused her delicate youth with drugs or minerals
That weaken motion: I 'll have 't disputed on;
'T is probable and palpable to thinking.
I therefore apprehend and do attach thee
For an abuser of the world, a practiser
Of arts inhibited and out of warrant.
Lay hold upon him: if he do resist,   80
Subdue him at his peril.

   Oth.   Hold your hands,
Both you of my inclining, and the rest:
Were it my cue to fight, I should have known it
Without a prompter.   Where will you that I go
To answer this your charge?

   Bra.   To prison, till fit time
Of law and course of direct session
Call thee to answer.

   Oth.   What if I do obey?
How may the duke be therewith satisfied,
Whose messengers are here about my side,
Upon some present business of the state   90
To bring me to him?

First Off.   'T is true, most worthy signior;
The duke 's in council, and your noble self,
I am sure, is sent for.

Bra.   How! the duke in council!
In this time of the night!   Bring him away:
Mine 's not an idle cause: the duke himself,
Or any of my brothers of the state,
Cannot but feel this wrong as 't were their own;
For if such actions may have passage free,
Bond-slaves and pagans shall our statesmen be.

[Exeunt.

SCENE III — *A council-chamber*

The DUKE *and* Senators *sitting at a table;*
Officers *attending*

Duke.   There is no composition in these news
That gives them credit.

First Sen.   Indeed, they are disproportion'd;
My letters say a hundred and seven galleys.

Duke.   And mine, a hundred and forty.

Sec. Sen.   And mine, two hundred:
But though they jump not on a just account, —
As in these cases, where the aim reports,
'T is oft with difference — yet do they all confirm
A Turkish fleet, and bearing up to Cyprus.

Duke.   Nay, it is possible enough to judgment:
I do not so secure me in the error,
But the main article I do approve
In fearful sense.

10

Sailor.   [*Within*] What, ho! what, ho! what, ho!

First Off.   A messenger from the galleys.

Enter a Sailor

Duke.   Now, what 's the business?
Sail.   The Turkish preparation makes for Rhodes;
So was I bid report here to the state
By Signior Angelo.
   Duke.   How say you by this change?
   First Sen.   This cannot be,
By no assay of reason; 't is a pageant,
To keep us in false gaze.   When we consider
The importancy of Cyprus to the Turk,   20
And let ourselves again but understand,
That as it more concerns the Turk than Rhodes,
So may he with more facile question bear it,
For that it stands not in such warlike brace,
But altogether lacks the abilities
That Rhodes is dress'd in: if we make thought of this,
We must not think the Turk is so unskilful
To leave that latest which concerns him first,
Neglecting an attempt of ease and gain,
To wake and wage a danger profitless.   30
   Duke.   Nay, in all confidence, he 's not for Rhodes.
   First Off.   Here is more news.

Enter a Messenger

   Mess.   The Ottomites, reverend and gracious,
Steering with due course towards the isle of Rhodes,
Have there injointed them with an after fleet.
   First Sen.   Ay, so I thought.   How many, as you
         guess?
   Mess.   Of thirty sail: and now they do re-stem
Their backward course, bearing with frank appearance

Their purposes toward Cyprus. Signior Montano,
Your trusty and most valiant servitor,   40
With his free duty recommends you thus,
And prays you to believe him.

    Duke. 'T is certain, then, for Cyprus.
Marcus Luccicos, is not he in town?

    First Sen. He 's now in Florence.

    Duke. Write from us to him; post-post-haste dis-
        patch.

    First Sen. Here comes Brabantio and the valiant
        Moor.

Enter BRABANTIO, OTHELLO, IAGO, RODERIGO, *and*
Officers

    Duke. Valiant Othello, we must straight employ
        you
Against the general enemy Ottoman.
[*To Brabantio*] I did not see you; welcome, gentle
        signior;   50
We lack'd your counsel and your help to-night.

    Bra. So did I yours. Good your grace, pardon me;
Neither my place nor aught I heard of business
Hath raised me from my bed, nor doth the general
        care
Take hold on me, for my particular grief
Is of so flood-gate and o'erbearing nature
That it engluts and swallows other sorrows
And it is still itself.

    Duke.   Why, what 's the matter?

    Bra. My daughter! O, my daughter!

    Duke and Sen.   Dead?

    Bra.   Ay, to me;

She is abused, stol'n from me, and corrupted   60
By spells and medicines bought of mountebanks
For nature so preposterously to err,
Being not deficient, blind, or lame of sense,
Sans witchcraft could not.

   Duke.   Whoe'er he be that in this foul proceeding
Hath thus beguiled your daughter of herself
And you of her, the bloody book of law
You shall yourself read in the bitter letter
After your own sense, yea, though our proper son
Stood in your action.

   Bra.   Humbly I thank your grace.   70
Here is the man, this Moor, whom now, it seems,
Your special mandate for the state-affairs
Hath hither brought.

   Duke and Sen.   We are very sorry for 't.

   Duke.   [*To Othello*] What, in your own part, can
        you say to this?

   Bra.   Nothing, but this is so.

   Oth.   Most potent, grave, and reverend signiors,
My very noble and approved good masters,
That I have ta'en away this old man's daughter,
It is most true; true, I have married her:
The very head and front of my offending   80
Hath this extent, no more.   Rude am I in my speech,
And little bless'd with the soft phrase of peace:
For since these arms of mine had seven years' pith,
Till now some nine moons wasted, they have used
Their dearest action in the tented field;
And little of this great world can I speak,
More than pertains to feats of broil and battle,
And therefore little shall I grace my cause

In speaking for myself. Yet, by your gracious
            patience,
I will a round unvarnish'd tale deliver   90
Of my whole course of love; what drugs, what
            charms,
What conjuration and what mighty magic —
For such proceeding I am charged withal —
I won his daughter.
    Bra.   A maiden never bold;
Of spirit so still and quiet, that her motion
Blush'd at herself; and she — in spite of nature,
Of years, of country, credit, every thing —
To fall in love with what she fear'd to look on!
It is a judgement maim'd and most imperfect
That will confess perfection so could err   100
Against all rules of nature, and must be driven
To find out practices of cunning hell,
Why this should be.   I therefore vouch again
That with some mixtures powerful o'er the blood,
Or with some dram conjured to this effect,
He wrought upon her.
    Duke.   To vouch this, is no proof,
Without more wider and more overt test
Than these thin habits and poor likelihoods
Of modern seeming do prefer against him.
    First Sen.   But, Othello, speak: 110
Did you by indirect and forced courses
Subdue and poison this young maid's affections?
Or came it by request and such fair question
As soul to soul affordeth?
    Oth.   I do beseech you,
Send for the lady to the Sagittary,

And let her speak of me before her father:
If you do find me foul in her report,
The trust, the office I do hold of you,
Not only take away, but let your sentence
Even fall upon my life.

    Duke.   Fetch Desdemona hither.   120

    Oth. Ancient, conduct them: you best know the
        place.   *[Exeunt Iago and Attendants.*

And, till she come, as truly as to heaven
I do confess the vices of my blood,
So justly to your grave ears I 'll present
How I did thrive in this fair lady's love,
And she in mine.

    Duke. Say it, Othello.

    Oth. Her father loved me; oft invited me;
Still question'd me the story of my life,
From year to year, the battles, sieges, fortunes,   130
That I have pass'd.
I ran it through, even from my boyish days,
To the very moment that he bade me tell it;
Wherein I spake of most disastrous chances,
Of moving accidents by flood and field,
Of hair-breadth scapes i' the imminent deadly breach,
Of being taken by the insolent foe
And sold to slavery, of my redemption thence
And portance in my travels' history:
Wherein of antres vast and deserts idle,   140
Rough quarries, rocks and hills whose heads touch
       heaven,
It was my hint to speak, — such was the process:
And of the Cannibals that each other eat,
The Anthropophagi, and men whose heads

Do grow beneath their shoulders. This to hear
Would Desdemona seriously incline:
But still the house-affairs would draw her thence:
Which ever as she could with haste dispatch,
She 'ld come again, and with a greedy ear
Devour up my discourse: which I observing,　　　150
Took once a pliant hour, and found good means
To draw from her a prayer of earnest heart
That I would all my pilgrimage dilate,
Whereof by parcels she had something heard,
But not intentively: I did consent,
And often did beguile her of her tears,
When I did speak of some distressful stroke
That my youth suffer'd. My story being done,
She gave me for my pains a world of sighs:
She swore, in faith, 't was strange, 't was passing
　　　　　strange,　　　160
'T was pitiful, 't was wondrous pitiful:
She wish'd she had not heard it, yet she wish'd
That heaven had made her such a man: she thank'd
　　　　me,
And bade me, if I had a friend that loved her,
I should but teach him how to tell my story,
And that would woo her. Upon this hint I spake:
She loved me for the dangers I had pass'd,
And I loved her that she did pity them.
This only is the witchcraft I have used:
Here comes the lady; let her witness it.　　　170

　　　　Enter DESDEMONA, IAGO, *and* attendants

　Duke. I think this tale would win my daughter
　　　too.

Good Brabantio,
Take up this mangled matter at the best:
Men do their broken weapons rather use
Than their bare hands.
    Bra.   I pray you, hear her speak:
If she confess that she was half the wooer,
Destruction on my head, if my bad blame
Light on the man! Come hither, gentle mis-
      tress:
Do you perceive in all this noble company
Where most you owe obedience?
    Des.   My noble father,   180
I do perceive here a divided duty:
To you I am bound for life and education;
My life and education both do learn me
How to respect you; you are the lord of duty;
I am hitherto your daughter: but here 's my hus-
      band,
And so much duty as my mother show'd
To you, preferring you before her father,
So much I challenge that I may profess
Due to the Moor my lord.
    Bra.   God be wi' you! I have done.
Please it your grace, on to the state-affairs: 190
I had rather to adopt a child than get it.
Come hither, Moor:
I here do give thee that with all my heart
Which, but thou hast already, with all my heart
I would keep from thee. For your sake, jewel,
I am glad at soul I have no other child;
For thy escape would teach me tyranny,
To hang clogs on them. I have done, my lord.

Duke. Let me speak like yourself, and lay a sen-
          tence,
Which, as a grise or step, may help these lovers   200
Into your favour.
When remedies are past, the griefs are ended
By seeing the worst, which late on hopes depended.
To mourn a mischief that is past and gone
Is the next way to draw new mischief on.
What cannot be preserved when fortune takes,
Patience her injury a mockery makes.
The robb'd that smiles steals something from the thief;
He robs himself that spends a bootless grief.

Bra. So let the Turk of Cyprus us beguile;   210
We lose it not, so long as we can smile.
He bears the sentence well that nothing bears
But the free comfort which from thence he hears,
But he bears both the sentence and the sorrow
That, to pay grief, must of patience borrow.
These sentences, to sugar, or to gall,
Being strong on both sides, are equivocal:
But words are words; I never yet did hear
That the bruised heart was pierced through the ear.
I humbly beseech you, proceed to the affairs of   220
          state.

Duke. The Turk with a most mighty preparation
makes for Cyprus. Othello, the fortitude of the
place is best known to you; and though we have
there a substitute of most allowed sufficiency, yet
opinion, a sovereign mistress of effects, throws a
more safer voice on you: you must therefore be
content to slubber the gloss of your new fortunes
with this more stubborn and boisterous expedition.

Oth.   The tyrant custom, most grave senators,   230
Hath made the flinty and steel couch of war
My thrice-driven bed of down: I do agnize
A natural and prompt alacrity
I find in hardness, and do undertake
These present wars against the Ottomites.
Most humbly therefore bending to your state,
I crave fit disposition for my wife,
Due reference of place and exhibition,
With such accommodation and besort
As levels with her breeding.

Duke.   If you please,   240
Be 't at her father's.

Bra.   I 'll not have it so.

Oth.   Nor I.

Des.   Nor I; I would not there reside,
To put my father in impatient thoughts
By being in his eye.   Most gracious duke,
To my unfolding lend your prosperous ear,
And let me find a charter in your voice,
To assist my simpleness.

Duke.   What would you, Desdemona?

Des.   That I did love the Moor to live with
            him,
My downright violence and storm of fortunes   250
May trumpet to the world: my heart's subdued
Even to the very quality of my lord:
I saw Othello's visage in his mind,
And to his honours and his valiant parts
Did I my soul and fortunes consecrate.
So that, dear lords, if I be left behind,
A moth of peace, and he go to the war,

The rites for which I love him are bereft me,
And I a heavy interim shall support
By his dear absence.   Let me go with him.   260

   Oth.   Let her have your voices.
Vouch with me, heaven, I therefore beg it not,
To please the palate of my appetite,
Nor to comply with heat — the young affects
In me defunct — and proper satisfaction,
But to be free and bounteous to her mind:
And heaven defend your good souls, that you think
I will your serious and great business scant
For she is with me: no, when light-wing'd toys
Of feather'd Cupid seel with wanton dullness   270
My speculative and officed instruments,
That my disports corrupt and taint my business,
Let housewives make a skillet of my helm,
And all indign and base adversities
Make head against my estimation!

   Duke.   Be it as you shall privately determine,
Either for her stay or going: the affair cries haste,
And speed must answer it.

   First Sen.   You must away to-night.

   Oth.   With all my heart.

   Duke.   At nine i' the morning here we'll meet
      again.
Othello, leave some officer behind,   281
And he shall our commission bring to you;
With such things else of quality and respect
As doth import you.

   Oth.   So please your grace, my ancient;
A man he is of honesty and trust:
To his conveyance I assign my wife,

With what else needful your good grace shall think
To be sent after me.

   Duke.   Let it be so.
Good night to every one. [*To Brab.*] And, noble
        signior,
If virtue no delighted beauty lack,   290
Your son-in-law is far more fair than black.

   First Sen.   Adieu, brave Moor; use Desdemona
      well.

   Bra.   Look to her, Moor, if thou hast eyes to see:
She has deceived her father, and may thee.

            [*Exeunt Duke, Senators, Officers, &c.*

   Oth.   My life upon her faith! Honest Iago,
My Desdemona must I leave to thee:
I prithee, let thy wife attend on her;
And bring them after in the best advantage.
Come, Desdemona: I have but an hour
Of love, of worldly matters and direction,   300
To spend with thee: we must obey the time.

           [*Exeunt Othello and Desdemona.*

   Rod.   Iago, —

   Iago.   What say'st thou, noble heart?

   Rod.   What will I do, thinkest thou?

   Iago.   Why, go to bed, and sleep.

   Rod.   I will incontinently drown myself.

   Iago.   If thou dost, I shall never love thee after.
Why, thou silly gentleman!

   Rod.   It is silliness to live when to live is torment;
and then have we a prescription to die when death
is our physician.   311

   Iago.   O villanous! I have looked upon the world
for four times seven years; and since I could distin-

guish betwixt a benefit and an injury, I never found
man that knew how to love himself. Ere I would say
I would drown myself for the love of a guinea-hen,
I would change my humanity with a baboon.

Rod. What should I do? I confess it is my shame
to be so fond; but it is not in my virtue to amend it. 321

Iago. Virtue! a fig! 't is in ourselves that we are
thus or thus. Our bodies are gardens, to the which
our wills are gardeners; so that if we will plant nettles
or sow lettuce, set hyssop and weed up thyme, supply
it with one gender of herbs or distract it with many,
either to have it sterile with idleness or manured
with industry, why, the power and corrigible authority of this lies in our wills. If the balance of our
lives had not one scale of reason to poise another of
sensuality, the blood and baseness of our natures
would conduct us to most preposterous conclusions:
but we have reason to cool our raging motions, our
carnal stings, our unbitted lusts, whereof I take this
that you call love to be a sect or scion.   337

Rod. It cannot be.

Iago. It is merely a lust of the blood and a per-
mission of the will. Come, be a man. Drown thyself! drown cats and blind puppies. I have professed
me thy friend, and I confess me knit to thy deserving
with cables of perdurable toughness; I could never
better stead thee than now. Put money in thy purse;
follow thou the wars; defeat thy favour with an
usurped beard; I say, put money in thy purse. It
cannot be that Desdemona should long continue her
love to the Moor — put money in thy purse — nor
he his to her: it was a violent commencement, and

thou shalt see an answerable sequestration; — put but money in thy purse. These Moors are changeable in their wills: — fill thy purse with money: — the food that to him now is as luscious as locusts, shall be to him shortly as bitter as coloquintida. She must change for youth: when she is sated with his body, she will find the error of her choice: she must have change, she must: therefore put money in thy purse. If thou wilt needs damn thyself, do it a more delicate way than drowning. Make all the money thou canst: if sanctimony and a frail vow betwixt an erring barbarian and a supersubtle Venetian be not too hard for my wits and all the tribe of hell, thou shalt enjoy her; therefore make money. A pox of drowning thyself! it is clean out of the way: seek thou rather to be hanged in compassing thy joy than to be drowned and go without her.

Rod.   Wilt thou be fast to my hopes, if I depend on the issue?   370

Iago.   Thou art sure of me: go, make money: I have told thee often, and I re-tell thee again and again, I hate the Moor: my cause is hearted; thine hath no less reason. Let us be conjunctive in our revenge against him: if thou canst cuckold him, thou dost thyself a pleasure, me a sport. There are many events in the womb of time which will be delivered. Traverse! go; provide thy money. We will have more of this to-morrow. Adieu.   380

Rod.   Where shall we meet i' the morning?

Iago.   At my lodging.

Rod.   I'll be with thee betimes.

Iago.   Go to; farewell. Do you hear, Roderigo?

 Rod. What say you?

 Iago. No more of drowning, do you hear?

 Rod. I am changed: I 'll go sell all my land. [*Exit.*

 Iago. Thus do I ever make my fool my purse;

For I mine own gain'd knowledge should profane, 390

If I would time expend with such a snipe,

But for my sport and profit. I hate the Moor;

And it is thought abroad, that 'twixt my sheets

He has done my office: I know not if 't be true;

But I, for mere suspicion in that kind,

Will do as if for surety. He holds me well;

The better shall my purpose work on him.

Cassio 's a proper man: let me see now:

To get his place and to plume up my will

In double knavery — How, how? — Let 's see: — 400

After some time, to abuse Othello's ear

That he is too familiar with his wife.

He hath a person and a smooth dispose

To be suspected, framed to make women false.

The Moor is of a free and open nature,

That thinks men honest that but seem to be so,

And will as tenderly be led by the nose

As asses are.

I have 't. It is engender'd. Hell and night

Must bring this monstrous birth to the world's light. 410

            [*Exit.*

ACT II

Scene I — *A Sea-port in Cyprus.   An open place near the quay*

Enter Montano *and two* Gentlemen

Mon.   What from the cape can you discern at sea?

First Gent.   Nothing at all: it is a high-wrought flood;

I cannot, 'twixt the heaven and the main,

Descry a sail.

Mon.   Methinks the wind hath spoke aloud at land;

A fuller blast ne'er shook our battlements:

If it hath ruffian'd so upon the sea,

What ribs of oak, when mountains melt on them,

Can hold the mortise?   What shall we hear of this?

Sec. Gent.   A segregation of the Turkish fleet: 10

For do but stand upon the foaming shore,

The chidden billow seems to pelt the clouds;

The wind-shaked surge, with high and monstrous mane,

Seems to cast water on the burning bear,

And quench the guards of the ever-fixed pole:

I never did like molestation view

On the enchafed flood.

Mon.   If that the Turkish fleet

Be not enshelter'd and embay'd, they are drown'd;

It is impossible they bear it out.

Enter a third Gentleman

Third Gent.   News, lads! our wars are done.   20

The desperate tempest hath so bang'd the Turks,

That their designment halts: a noble ship of Venice
Hath seen a grievous wreck and suffrance
On most part of their fleet.

   Mon.   How! is this true?

   Third Gent.   The ship is here put in,
A Veronesa; Michael Cassio,
Lieutenant to the warlike Moor Othello,
Is come on shore: the Moor himself at sea,
And is in full commission here for Cyprus.

   Mon.   I am glad on 't: 't is a worthy governor.   30

   Third Gent.   But this same Cassio, though he
         speak of comfort
Touching the Turkish loss, yet he looks sadly,
And prays the Moor be safe; for they were parted
With foul and violent tempest.

   Mon.   Pray heavens he be;
For I have served him, and the man commands
Like a full soldier.   Let 's to the seaside, ho!
As well to see the vessel that 's come in
As to throw out our eyes for brave Othello,
Even till we make the main and the aerial blue
An indistinct regard.

   Third Gent.   Come, let 's do so;   40
For every minute is expectancy
Of more arrivance.

Enter CASSIO

   Cas.   Thanks, you the valiant of this warlike isle,
That so approve the Moor!   O, let the heavens
Give him defence against the elements,
For I have lost him on a dangerous sea.

   Mon.   Is he well shipp'd?

   Cas.   His bark is stoutly timber'd, and his pilot

Of very expert and approved allowance;
Therefore my hopes, not surfeited to death,   50
Stand in bold cure.

        [*A cry within* "A sail, a sail, a sail!"

        Enter a fourth Gentleman

    Cas.   What noise?
    Fourth Gent.   The town is empty; on the brow o'
       the sea
Stand ranks of people, and they cry "A sail!"
    Cas.   My hopes do shape him for the governor.
                        [*Guns heard.*
    Sec. Gent.   They do discharge their shot of courtesy:
Our friends at least.
    Cas.   I pray you, sir, go forth,
And give us truth who 't is that is arrived.
    Sec. Gent.   I shall.   [*Exit.*
    Mon.   But, good lieutenant, is your general wived?   60
    Cas.   Most fortunately: he hath achieved a maid
That paragons description and wild fame;
One that excels the quirks of blazoning pens,
And in the essential vesture of creation
Does tire the ingener.

        Re-enter second Gentleman

             How now! who has put in?
    Sec. Gent.   'T is one Iago, ancient to the general.
    Cas.   Has had most favourable and happy speed:
Tempests themselves, high seas and howling winds,
The gutter'd rocks and congregated sands, —
Traitors ensteep'd to clog the guiltless keel, —   70
As having sense of beauty, do omit

Their mortal natures, letting go safely by
The divine Desdemona.

 Mon.   What is she?

 Cas. She that I spake of, our great captain's
     captain,
Left in the conduct of the bold Iago,
Whose footing here anticipates our thoughts
A se'nnight's speed. Great Jove, Othello guard,
And swell his sail with thine own powerful breath,
That he may bless this bay with his tall ship,
Make love's quick pants in Desdemona's arms,   80
Give renew'd fire to our extincted spirits,
And bring all Cyprus comfort!

   Enter DESDEMONA, EMILIA, IAGO, RODERIGO,
       and Attendants

            O, behold,
The riches of the ship is come on shore!
Ye men of Cyprus, let her have your knees.
Hail to thee, lady! and the grace of heaven,
Before, behind thee, and on every hand,
Enwheel thee round!

 Des.   I thank you, valiant Cassio.
What tidings can you tell me of my lord?

 Cas. He is not yet arrived: nor know I aught
But that he 's well and will be shortly here.   90

 Des. O, but I fear — How lost you company?

 Cas. The great contention of the sea and skies
Parted our fellowship — But, hark! a sail.

    [*A cry within* "A sail, a sail!" *Guns heard.*

 Sec. Gent. They give their greeting to the citadel:
This likewise is a friend.

Cas.   See for the news.   [*Exit Gentleman.*

Good ancient, you are welcome.   [*To Emilia*]   Wel-
          come, mistress:

Let it not gall your patience, good Iago,

That I extend my manners; 't is my breeding

That gives me this bold show of courtesy.   100

                    [*Kissing her.*

Iago.   Sir, would she give you so much of her lips

As of her tongue she oft bestows on me,

You 'ld have enough.

Des.   Alas, she has no speech.

Iago.   In faith, too much;

I find it still, when I have list to sleep:

Marry, before your ladyship, I grant,

She puts her tongue a little in her heart,

And chides with thinking.

Emil.   You have little cause to say so.

Iago.   Come on, come on; you are pictures out of
          doors,   110

Bells in your parlours, wild-cats in your kitchens,

Saints in your injuries, devils being offended,

Players in your housewifery, and housewives in your
          beds.

Des.   O, fie upon thee, slanderer!

Iago.   Nay, it is true, or else I am a Turk:

You rise to play and go to bed to work.

Emil.   You shall not write my praise.

Iago.   No, let me not.

Des.   What wouldst thou write of me, if thou
          shouldst praise me?

Iago.   O gentle lady, do not put me to 't;

For I am nothing, if not critical.   120

Des. Come on, assay — There's one gone to the
  harbour?

Iago. Ay, madam.

Des. I am not merry; but I do beguile
The thing I am by seeming otherwise.
Come, how wouldst thou praise me?

Iago. I am about it; but indeed my invention
Comes from my pate as birdlime does from frize;
It plucks out brains and all: but my Muse labours,
And thus she is deliver'd.
If she be fair and wise, fairness and wit,   130
The one's for use, the other useth it.

Des. Well praised! How if she be black and
  witty?

Iago. If she be black, and thereto have a wit,
She 'll find a white that shall her blackness fit.

Des. Worse and worse.

Emil. How if fair and foolish?

Iago. She never yet was foolish that was fair;
For even her folly help'd her to an heir.

Des. These are old fond paradoxes to make fools
laugh i' the alehouse. What miserable praise hast
thou for her that 's foul and foolish?   141

Iago. There 's none so foul and foolish thereunto,
But does foul pranks which fair and wise ones do.

Des. O heavy ignorance! thou praisest the worst
best. But what praise couldst thou bestow on a
deserving woman indeed, one that, in the authority
of her merit, did justly put on the vouch of very
malice itself?

Iago. She that was ever fair and never proud,
Had tongue at will and yet was never loud,   150

Never lack'd gold and yet went never gay,
Fled from her wish and yet said "Now I may,"
She that being anger'd, her revenge being nigh,
Bade her wrong stay and her displeasure fly,
She that in wisdom never was so frail
To change the cod's head for the salmon's tail,
She that could think and ne'er disclose her mind,
See suitors following and not look behind,
She was a wight, if ever such wight were, —

Des. To do what?   160

Iago.   To suckle fools and chronicle small beer.

Des. O most lame and impotent conclusion! Do
not learn of him, Emilia, though he be thy husband.
How say you, Cassio? is he not a most profane and
liberal counsellor?

Cas. He speaks home, madam: you may relish
him more in the soldier than in the scholar.   167

Iago. [*Aside*] He takes her by the palm: ay,
well said, whisper: with as little a web as this will I
ensnare as great a fly as Cassio. Ay, smile upon her,
do; I will gyve thee in thine own courtship. You
say true; 't is so, indeed: if such tricks as these
strip you out of your lieutenantry, it had been better
you had not kissed your three fingers so oft, which
now again you are most apt to play the sir in. Very
good; well kissed! an excellent courtesy! 't is so,
indeed. Yet again your fingers to your lips? would
they were clyster-pipes for your sake! [*Trumpet
within.*] The Moor! I know his trumpet.

Cas. 'T is truly so.   181

Des. Let 's meet him and receive him.

Cas. Lo, where he comes!

Enter OTHELLO *and* Attendants

Oth.   O my fair warrior!

Des.   My dear Othello!

Oth.   It gives me wonder great as my content
To see you here before me.   O my soul's joy!
If after every tempest come such calms,
May the winds blow till they have waken'd death!
And let the labouring bark climb hills of seas
Olympus-high and duck again as low   190
As hell 's from heaven!   If it were now to die,
'T were now to be most happy; for I fear,
My soul hath her content so absolute
That not another comfort like to this
Succeeds in unknown fate.

Des.   The heavens forbid
But that our loves and comforts should increase,
Even as our days do grow!

Oth.   Amen to that, sweet powers!
I cannot speak enough of this content;
It stops me here; it is too much of joy:
And this, and this, the greatest discords be   200

                              [*Kissing her.*

That e'er our hearts shall make!

Iago.   [*Aside*]   O, you are well tuned now!
But I 'll set down the pegs that make this music,
As honest as I am.

Oth.   Come, let us to the castle.
News, friends; our wars are done, the Turks are
          drown'd.
How does my old acquaintance of this isle?
Honey, you shall be well desired in Cyprus;

I have found great love amongst them.   O my sweet,
I prattle out of fashion, and I dote
In mine own comforts.   I prithee, good Iago,
Go to the bay and disembark my coffers: 210
Bring thou the master to the citadel;
He is a good one, and his worthiness
Does challenge much respect.   Come, Desdemona,
Once more, well met at Cyprus.

       [Exeunt Othello, Desdemona, and Attendants.

    Iago.   Do thou meet me presently at the harbour.
Come hither.   If thou be'st valiant, — as, they say,
base men being in love have then a nobility in their
natures more than is native to them, — list me.   The
lieutenant to-night watches on the court of guard.
First, I must tell thee this: Desdemona is directly
in love with him.

    Rod.   With him! why, 't is not possible.   222

    Iago.   Lay thy finger thus, and let thy soul be
instructed.   Mark me with what violence she first
loved the Moor, but for bragging and telling her fan-
tastical lies: and will she love him still for prating?
let not thy discreet heart think it.   Her eye must
be fed; and what delight shall she have to look on
the devil?   When the blood is made dull with the act
of sport, there should be, again to inflame it and to
give satiety a fresh appetite, loveliness in favour,
sympathy in years, manners and beauties; all which
the Moor is defective in: now, for want of these
required conveniences, her delicate tenderness will
find itself abused, begin to heave the gorge, dis-
relish and abhor the Moor; very nature will instruct
her in it and compel her to some second choice.   Now,

sir, this granted, — as it is a most pregnant and
unforced position — who stands so eminent in the
degree of this fortune as Cassio does? a knave very
voluble; no further conscionable than in putting on
the mere form of civil and humane seeming, for the
better compassing of his salt and most hidden loose
affection? why, none; why, none: a slipper and
subtle knave, a finder of occasions, that has an eye
can stamp and counterfeit advantages, though true
advantage never present itself; a devilish knave.
Besides, the knave is handsome, young, and hath
all those requisites in him that folly and green minds
look after: a pestilent complete knave; and the
woman hath found him already.

Rod. I cannot believe that in her; she's full of
most blessed condition.

Iago. Blessed fig's-end! the wine she drinks is
made of grapes: if she had been blessed, she would
never have loved the Moor. Blessed pudding!
Didst thou not see her paddle with the palm of his
hand? didst not mark that?   260

Rod. Yes, that I did; but that was but courtesy.

Iago. L   ry, by this hand; an index and obscure
prologue   he history of lust and foul thoughts.
They me   near with their lips that their breaths
embraced together. Villanous thoughts, Roderigo!
when these mutualities so marshal the way, hard at
hand comes the master and main exercise, the incor-
porate conclusion. Pish! But, sir, be you ruled by
    : I have brought you from Venice. Watch you
to-night; for the command, I'll lay't upon you.
Cassio knows you not. I'll not be far from you:

do you find some occasion to anger Cassio, either
by speaking too loud, or tainting his discipline; or
from what other course you please, which the time
shall more favourably minister.   276

    Rod. Well.

    Iago. Sir, he is rash and very sudden in choler,
and haply may strike at you: provoke him, that he
may; for even out of that will I cause these of
Cyprus to mutiny; whose qualification shall come
into no true taste again but by the displanting of
Cassio. So shall you have a shorter journey to your
desires by the means I shall then have to prefer
them; and the impediment most profitably removed,
without the which there were no expectation of our
prosperity.   289

    Rod. I will do this, if I can bring it to any oppor-
        tunity.

    Iago. I warrant thee. Meet me by and by at
the citadel: I must fetch his necessaries ashore.
Farewell.

    Rod. Adieu.   [*Exit.*

    Iago. That Cassio loves her, I do well believe it;
That she loves him, 't is apt and of great credit:
The Moor, howbeit that I endure him not,
Is of a constant, loving, noble nature,
And I dare think he 'll prove to Desdemona
A most dear husband. Now, I do love her too;   300
Not out of absolute lust, though peradventure
I stand accountant for as great a sin,
But partly led to diet my revenge,
For that I do suspect the lusty Moor
Hath leap'd into my seat; the thought whereof

Doth, like a poisonous mineral, gnaw my inwards;
And nothing can or shall content my soul
Till I am even'd with him, wife for wife,
Or failing so, yet that I put the Moor
At least into a jealousy so strong   310
That judgement cannot cure.   Which thing to do,
If this poor trash of Venice, whom I trash
For his quick hunting, stand the putting on,
I 'll have our Michael Cassio on the hip,
Abuse him to the Moor in the rank garb —
For I fear Cassio with my night-cap too —
Make the Moor thank me, love me and reward me,
For making him egregiously an ass
And practising upon his peace and quiet
Even to madness.   'T is here, but yet confused.   320
Knavery's plain face is never seen till used.   [*Exit.*

SCENE II — *A street*

Enter a Herald *with a proclamation;* People *following*

Her.   It is Othello's pleasure, our noble and valiant general, that, upon certain tidings now arrived,
importing the mere perdition of the Turkish fleet,
every man put himself into triumph; some to dance,
some to make bonfires, each man to what sport and
revels his addiction leads him: for, besides these
beneficial news, it is the celebration of his nuptial.
So much was his pleasure should be proclaimed.   All
offices are open, and there is full liberty of feasting
from this present hour of five till the bell have told
eleven.   Heaven bless the isle of Cyprus and our
noble general Othello!   [*Exeunt.*

Scene III — *A hall in the castle*

Enter Othello, Desdemona, Cassio, *and* Attendants

Oth.   Good Michael, look you to the guard to-
       night:
Let 's teach ourselves that honourable stop,
Not to outsport discretion.
    Cas.   Iago hath direction what to do;
But, notwithstanding, with my personal eye
Will I look to 't.
    Oth.   Iago is most honest.
Michael, good night: to-morrow with your earliest
Let me have speech with you. [*To Desdemona*]
       Come, my dear love,
The purchase made, the fruits are to ensue;
That profit 's yet to come 'tween me and you.   10
Good night.
    [*Exeunt Othello, Desdemona, and Attendants.*

Enter Iago

    Cas.   Welcome, Iago; we must to the watch.
    Iago.   Not this hour, lieutenant; 't is not yet
ten o' the clock. Our general cast us thus early
for the love of his Desdemona; who let us not therefore blame: he hath not yet made wanton the night
with her; and she is sport for Jove.
    Cas.   She 's a most exquisite lady.
    Iago.   And, I 'll warrant her, full of game.   20
    Cas.   Indeed, she 's a most fresh and delicate
creature.
    Iago.   What an eye she has! methinks it sounds
a parley of provocation.

Cas. An inviting eye; and yet methinks right modest.

Iago. And when she speaks, is it not an alarum to love?

Cas. She is indeed perfection.

Iago. Well, happiness to their sheets! Come, lieutenant, I have a stoup of wine; and here without are a brace of Cyprus gallants that would fain have a measure to the health of black Othello.

Cas. Not to-night, good Iago: I have very poor and unhappy brains for drinking: I could well wish courtesy would invent some other custom of entertainment.

Iago. O, they are our friends; but one cup: I 'll drink for you.   39

Cas. I have drunk but one cup to-night, and that was craftily qualified too, and, behold, what innovation it makes here: I am unfortunate in the infirmity, and dare not task my weakness with any more.

Iago. What, man! 't is a night of revels: the gallants desire it.

Cas. Where are they?

Iago. Here at the door; I pray you, call them in.

Cas. I 'll do 't; but it dislikes me.   [*Exit.*

Iago. If I can fasten but one cup upon him,   50
With that which he hath drunk to-night already,
He 'll be as full of quarrel and offence
As my young mistress' dog. Now, my sick fool
        Roderigo,
Whom love hath turn'd almost the wrong side out,

To Desdemona hath to-night caroused
Potations pottle-deep; and he 's to watch:
Three lads of Cyprus, noble swelling spirits,
That hold their honours in a wary distance,
The very elements of this warlike isle,
Have I to-night fluster'd with flowing cups,　　60
And they watch too.　Now, 'mongst this flock of
　　　　drunkards,
Am I to put our Cassio in some action
That may offend the isle. — But here they come:
If consequence do but approve my dream,
My boat sails freely, both with wind and stream.

Re-enter CASSIO; *with him* MONTANO *and* Gentlemen;
　　　Servants *following with wine*

　Cas.　'Fore God, they have given me a rouse
already.
　Mon.　Good faith, a little one; not past a pint,
as I am a soldier.
　Iago.　Some wine, ho!　　　　　　70
[*Sings*]　And let me the canakin clink, clink;
　　　　And let me the canakin clink:
　　　　　A soldier's a man;
　　　　　A life's but a span;
　　　　Why, then, let a soldier drink.
Some wine, boys!
　Cas.　'Fore God, an excellent song.
　Iago.　I learned it in England, where, indeed,
they are most potent in potting: your Dane, your
German, and your swag-bellied Hollander — Drink,
ho! — are nothing to your English.　　　81

Cas. Is your Englishman so expert in his drinking?

Iago. Why, he drinks you, with facility, your Dane dead drunk; he sweats not to overthrow your Almain; he gives your Hollander a vomit, ere the next pottle can be filled.

Cas. To the health of our general!

Mon. I am for it, lieutenant; and I 'll do you justice.

Iago. O sweet England! 91

    King Stephen was a worthy peer,
      His breeches cost him but a crown;
    He held them sixpence all too dear,
      With that he call'd the tailor lown.
    He was a wight of high renown,
      And thou art but of low degree:
    'T is pride that pulls the country down;
      Then take thine auld cloak about thee.

Some wine, ho! 100

Cas. Why, this is a more exquisite song than the other.

Iago. Will you hear 't again?

Cas. No; for I hold him to be unworthy of his place that does those things. Well, God's above all; and there be souls must be saved, and there be souls must not be saved.

Iago. It 's true, good lieutenant.

Cas. For mine own part, — no offence to the general, nor any man of quality, — I hope to be saved. 111

Iago. And so do I too, lieutenant.

Cas. Ay, but, by your leave, not before me; the lieutenant is to be saved before the ancient. Let 's

have no more of this; let's to our affairs. God
forgive us our sins! Gentlemen, let's look to our
business. Do not think, gentlemen, I am drunk:
this is my ancient; this is my right hand, and this
is my left: I am not drunk now; I can stand well
enough, and speak well enough.   120

   All. Excellent well.

   Cas. Why, very well then; you must not think
then that I am drunk.   [*Exit.*

   Mon. To the platform, masters; come, let's set
the watch.

   Iago. You see this fellow that is gone before;
He is a soldier fit to stand by Cæsar
And give direction: and do but see his vice;
'T is to his virtue a just equinox,
The one as long as the other: 't is pity of him.   130
I fear the trust Othello puts him in,
On some odd time of his infirmity,
Will shake this island.

   Mon.   But is he often thus?

   Iago. 'T is evermore the prologue to his sleep:
He 'll watch the horologe a double set,
If drink rock not his cradle.

   Mon.   It were well
The general were put in mind of it.
Perhaps he sees it not, or his good nature
Prizes the virtue that appears in Cassio,
And looks not on his evils: is not this true?   140

Enter Roderigo

   Iago. [*Aside to him*] How now, Roderigo!
I pray you, after the lieutenant; go. [*Exit Roderigo.*

Mon. And 't is great pity that the noble Moor
Should hazard such a place as his own second
With one of an ingraft infirmity:
It were an honest action to say
So to the Moor.

Iago. Not I, for this fair island:
I do love Cassio well; and would do much
To cure him of this evil — But, hark! what noise?
[*Cry within:* "Help! help!"]

Re-enter Cassio, *driving in* Roderigo

Cas. You rogue! you rascal!
Mon. What 's the matter, lieutenant?
Cas. A knave teach me my duty!   151
I 'll beat the knave into a twiggen bottle.
Rod. Beat me!
Cas. Dost thou prate, rogue? [*Striking Roderigo.*
Mon. Nay, good lieutenant; I pray you, sir, hold
your hand.   [*Staying him.*
Cas. Let me go, sir, or I 'll knock you o'er the
mazzard.
Mon. Come, come, you 're drunk.
Cas. Drunk!   [*They fight.*
Iago. [*Aside to Roderigo*] Away, I say; go out,
and cry a mutiny.   [*Exit Roderigo.*
Nay, good lieutenant! — God's will, gentlemen; —
Help, ho! — Lieutenant, — sir, — Montano, — sir; —
Help, masters! — Here 's a goodly watch indeed!
[*A bell rings.*
Who 's that which rings the bell? — Diablo, ho!
The town will rise: God 's will, lieutenant, hold!
You will be shamed for ever.

Re-enter Othello *and* Attendants

Oth.   What is the matter here?
Mon. 'Zounds, I bleed still; I am hurt to the
　　　　death.   [*Faints.*
Oth. Hold, for your lives!
Iago. Hold, ho! Lieutenant, — sir, — Montano,
　　　　—gentlemen,—

Have you forgot all sense of place and duty?
Hold! the general speaks to you; hold, hold, for
　　　shame!
Oth. Why, how now, ho! from whence ariseth
　　　this?
Are we turn'd Turks, and to ourselves do that   170
Which heaven hath forbid the Ottomites?
For Christian shame, put by this barbarous brawl:
He that stirs next to carve for his own rage
Holds his soul light; he dies upon his motion.
Silence that dreadful bell: it frights the isle
From her propriety.   What is the matter, masters?
Honest Iago, that look'st dead with grieving,
Speak, who began this? on thy love, I charge thee.
Iago. I do not know: friends all but now, even
　　　now,
In quarter, and in terms like bride and groom   180
Devesting them for bed; and then, but now,
As if some planet had unwitted men,
Swords out, and tilting one at other's breast,
In opposition bloody.   I cannot speak
Any beginning to this peevish odds;
And would in action glorious I had lost
Those legs that brought me to a part of it!

Oth.   How comes it, Michael, you are thus forgot?

Cas.   I pray you, pardon me; I cannot speak.

Oth.   Worthy Montano, you were wont be civil; 190
The gravity and stillness of your youth
The world hath noted, and your name is great
In mouths of wisest censure: what's the matter,
That you unlace your reputation thus
And spend your rich opinion for the name
Of a night-brawler? give me answer to it.

Mon.   Worthy Othello, I am hurt to danger:
Your officer, Iago, can inform you —
While I spare speech, which something now offends
          me —
Of all that I do know: nor know I aught   200
By me that's said or done amiss this night;
Unless self-charity be sometimes a vice,
And to defend ourselves it be a sin
When violence assails us.

Oth.   Now, by heaven,
My blood begins my safer guides to rule;
And passion, having my best judgement collied,
Assays to lead the way: if I once stir,
Or do but lift this arm, the best of you
Shall sink in my rebuke.   Give me to know
How this foul rout began, who set it on;   210
And he that is approved in this offence,
Though he had twinn'd with me, both at a birth,
Shall lose me.   What! in a town of war,
Yet wild, the people's hearts brimful of fear,
To manage private and domestic quarrel,
In night, and on the court and guard of safety!
'T is monstrous.   Iago, who began 't?

Mon. If partially affined, or leagued in office,
Thou dost deliver more or less than truth,
Thou art no soldier.

Iago.   Touch me not so near: 220
I had rather have this tongue cut from my mouth
Than it should do offence to Michael Cassio;
Yet, I persuade myself, to speak the truth
Shall nothing wrong him.   Thus it is, general.
Montano and myself being in speech,
There comes a fellow crying out for help;
And Cassio following him with determined sword,
To execute upon him.   Sir, this gentleman
Steps in to Cassio and entreats his pause:
Myself the crying fellow did pursue,   230
Lest by his clamour — as it so fell out —
The town might fall in fright: he, swift of foot,
Outran my purpose; and I return'd the rather
For that I heard the clink and fall of swords,
And Cassio high in oath; which till to-night
I ne'er might say before.   When I came back —
For this was brief — I found them close together,
At blow and thrust; even as again they were
When you yourself did part them.
More of this matter cannot I report: 240
But men are men; the best sometimes forget:
Though Cassio did some little wrong to him,
As men in rage strike those that wish them best,
Yet surely Cassio, I believe, received
From him that fled some strange indignity,
Which patience could not pass.

Oth.   I know, Iago,
Thy honesty and love doth mince this matter,

Making it light to Cassio.   Cassio, I love thee;
But never more be officer of mine.

Re-enter DESDEMONA, *attended*

Look, if my gentle love be not raised up!   250
I 'll make thee an example.

    Des.   What 's the matter?

    Oth.   All 's well now, sweeting; come away to bed.
Sir, for your hurts, myself will be your surgeon:
Lead him off.   [*To Montano, who is led off.*
Iago, look with care about the town,
And silence those whom this vile brawl distracted.
Come, Desdemona: 't is the soldiers' life
To have their balmy slumbers waked with strife.

            [*Exeunt all but Iago and Cassio.*

    Iago.   What, are you hurt, lieutenant?

    Cas.   Ay, past all surgery.   260

    Iago.   Marry, heaven forbid!

    Cas.   Reputation, reputation, reputation! O, I
have lost my reputation! I have lost the immortal
part of myself, and what remains is bestial. My
reputation, Iago, my reputation!

    Iago.   As I am an honest man, I thought you had
received some bodily wound; there is more sense in
that than in reputation. Reputation is an idle and
most false imposition: oft got without merit, and
lost without deserving: you have lost no reputation
at all, unless you repute yourself such a loser. What,
man! there are ways to recover the general again:
you are but now cast in his mood, a punishment
more in policy than in malice; even so as one would
beat his offenceless dog to affright an imperious lion:
sue to him again, and he 's yours.   277

Cas. I will rather sue to be despised than to deceive so good a commander with so slight, so drunken, and so indiscreet an officer. Drunk? and speak parrot? and squabble? swagger? swear? and discourse fustian with one's own shadow? O thou invisible spirit of wine, if thou hast no name to be known by, let us call thee devil!

Iago. What was he that you followed with your sword? What had he done to you?   286

Cas. I know not.

Iago. Is 't possible?

Cas. I remember a mass of things, but nothing distinctly; a quarrel, but nothing wherefore. O God, that men should put an enemy in their mouths to steal away their brains! that we should, with joy, pleasance, revel and applause, transform ourselves into beasts!

Iago. Why, but you are now well enough: how came you thus recovered?

Cas. It hath pleased the devil drunkenness to give place to the devil wrath: one unperfectness shows me another, to make me frankly despise myself.   300

Iago. Come, you are too severe a moraler: as the time, the place, and the condition of this country stands, I could heartily wish this had not befallen; but, since it is as it is, mend it for your own good.

Cas. I will ask him for my place again; he shall tell me I am a drunkard! Had I as many mouths as Hydra, such an answer would stop them all. To be now a sensible man, by and by a fool, and pres-

ently a beast! O strange! Every inordinate cup is
unblessed and the ingredient is a devil.   312

Iago. Come, come, good wine is a good familiar
creature, if it be well used: exclaim no more against
it. And, good lieutenant, I think you think I love you.

Cas. I have well approved it, sir. I drunk!

Iago. You or any man living may be drunk at
some time, man. I'll tell you what you shall do.
Our general's wife is now the general: I may say so
in this respect, for that he hath devoted and given
up himself to the contemplation, mark, and denote-
ment of her parts and graces: confess yourself freely
to her; importune her help to put you in your place
again: she is of so free, so kind, so apt, so blessed
a disposition, she holds it a vice in her goodness not
to do more than she is requested: this broken joint
between you and her husband entreat her to splinter;
and, my fortunes against any lay worth naming, this
crack of your love shall grow stronger than it was
before.   331

Cas. You advise me well.

Iago. I protest, in the sincerity of love and
honest kindness.

Cas. I think it freely; and betimes in the morning I will beseech the virtuous Desdemona to undertake for me: I am desperate of my fortunes if they
check me here.

Iago. You are in the right. Good night, lieu-
tenant; I must to the watch.   340

Cas. Good night, honest Iago.   [*Exit.*

Iago. And what's he then that says I play the
          villain?

When this advice is free I give and honest,
Probal to thinking, and indeed the course
To win the Moor again?   For 't is most easy
The inclining Desdemona to subdue
In any honest suit: she 's framed as fruitful
As the free elements.   And then for her
To win the Moor — were 't to renounce his baptism,
All seals and symbols of redeemed sin,   350
His soul is so enfetter'd to her love,
That she may make, unmake, do what she list,
Even as her appetite shall play the god
With his weak function.   How am I then a villain
To counsel Cassio to this parallel course,
Directly to his good?   Divinity of hell!
When devils will the blackest sins put on,
They do suggest at first with heavenly shows,
As I do now: for whiles this honest fool
Plies Desdemona to repair his fortunes   360
And she for him pleads strongly to the Moor,
I 'll pour this pestilence into his ear,
That she repeals him for her body's lust;
And by how much she strives to do him good,
She shall undo her credit with the Moor.
So will I turn her virtue into pitch,
And out of her own goodness make the net
That shall enmesh them all.

Re-enter RODERIGO

                              How now, Roderigo!
Rod.   I do follow here in the chase, not like a
hound that hunts, but one that fills up the cry.
My money is almost spent; I have been to-night

exceedingly well cudgelled; and I think the issue
will be, I shall have so much experience for my
pains, and so, with no money at all and a little more
wit, return again to Venice.

Iago.   How poor are they that have not patience!
What wound did ever heal but by degrees?
Thou know'st we work by wit, and not by witchcraft;
And wit depends on dilatory time.
Does 't not go well?   Cassio hath beaten thee,   380
And thou by that small hurt hast cashier'd Cassio:
Though other things grow fair against the sun,
Yet fruits that blossom first will first be ripe:
Content thyself awhile.   By the mass, 't is morning;
Pleasure and action make the hours seem short.
Retire thee; go where thou art billeted:
Away, I say; thou shalt know more hereafter:
Nay, get thee gone. [*Exit Roderigo.*]   Two things
          are to be done:
My wife must move for Cassio to her mistress;
I 'll set her on;   390
Myself the while to draw the Moor apart,
And bring him jump when he may Cassio find
Soliciting his wife: ay, that 's the way:
Dull not device by coldness and delay.   [*Exit.*

ACT III

Scene I — *Before the castle*

Enter Cassio *and some* Musicians

Cas. Masters, play here; I will content your
    pains;
Something that 's brief; and bid "Good morrow,
general."   [*Music.*

Enter Clown

Clo. Why, masters, have your instruments been
in Naples, that they speak i' the nose thus?

First Mus. How, sir, how!

Clo. Are these, I pray you, wind-instruments?

First Mus. Ay, marry, are they, sir.

Clo. O, thereby hangs a tail.

First Mus. Whereby hangs a tale, sir?   9

Clo. Marry, sir, by many a wind-instrument that
I know. But, masters, here 's money for you: and
the general so likes your music, that he desires you,
for love's sake, to make no more noise with it.

First Mus. Well, sir, we will not.

Clo. If you have any music that may not be
heard, to 't again: but, as they say, to hear music
the general does not greatly care.

First Mus. We have none such, sir.   19

Clo. Then put up your pipes in your bag, for I 'll
away: go; vanish into air; away! [*Exeunt Musicians.*

Cas. Dost thou hear, my honest friend?

Clo. No, I hear not your honest friend; I hear you.

Cas. Prithee, keep up thy quillets. There's a
poor piece of gold for thee: if the gentlewoman that

attends the general's wife be stirring, tell her there's
one Cassio entreats her a little favour of speech: wilt
thou do this?

Clo. She is stirring, sir: if she will stir hither, I
shall seem to notify unto her.   31

Cas. Do, good my friend.   *[Exit Clown.*

Enter Iago

                              In happy time, Iago.
Iago. You have not been a-bed, then?
Cas. Why, no; the day had broke
Before we parted.   I have made bold, Iago,
To send in to your wife: my suit to her
Is, that she will to virtuous Desdemona
Procure me some access.
Iago.   I 'll send her to you presently;
And I 'll devise a mean to draw the Moor
Out of the way, that your converse and business   40
May be more free.
Cas. I humbly thank you for 't.   *[Exit Iago.]*
          I never knew
A Florentine more kind and honest.

Enter Emilia

Emil. Good morrow, good lieutenant: I am sorry
For your displeasure; but all will sure be well.
The general and his wife are talking of it;
And she speaks for you stoutly: the Moor replies,
That he you hurt is of great fame in Cyprus
And great affinity, and that in wholesome wisdom
He might not but refuse you; but he protests he
          loves you,   50
And needs no other suitor but his likings

To take the safest occasion by the front
To bring you in again.

   Cas.   Yet, I beseech you,
If you think fit, or that it may be done,
Give me advantage of some brief discourse
With Desdemona alone.

   Emil.   Pray you, come in:
I will bestow you where you shall have time
To speak your bosom freely.

   Cas.   I am much bound to you.   [*Exeunt.*

SCENE II — *A room in the castle*

Enter OTHELLO, IAGO, *and* Gentlemen

   Oth.   These letters give, Iago, to the pilot;
And by him do my duties to the senate:
That done, I will be walking on the works;
Repair there to me.

   Iago.   Well, my good lord, I 'll do 't.

   Oth.   This fortification, gentlemen, shall we see 't?

   Gent.   We 'll wait upon your lordship.   [*Exeunt.*

SCENE III — *The garden of the castle*

Enter DESDEMONA, CASSIO, *and* EMILIA

   Des.   Be thou assured, good Cassio, I will do
All my abilities in thy behalf.

   Emil.   Good madam, do: I warrant it grieves my
              husband,
As if the case were his.

   Des.   O, that 's an honest fellow. Do not doubt,
              Cassio,
But I will have my lord and you again
As friendly as you were.

Cas.   Bounteous madam,
Whatever shall become of Michael Cassio,
He 's never any thing but your true servant.

    Des. I know 't; I thank you. You do love my
        lord: 10
You have known him long; and be you well assured
He shall in strangeness stand no further off
Than in a politic distance.

    Cas.   Ay, but, lady,
That policy may either last so long,
Or feed upon such nice and waterish diet,
Or breed itself so out of circumstance,
That, I being absent and my place supplied,
My general will forget my love and service.

    Des. Do not doubt that; before Emilia here
I give thee warrant of thy place: assure thee,   20
If I do vow a friendship, I 'll perform it
To the last article: my lord shall never rest:
I 'll watch him tame and talk him out of patience;
His bed shall seem a school, his board a shrift;
I 'll intermingle every thing he does
With Cassio's suit: therefore be merry, Cassio;
For thy solicitor shall rather die
Than give thy cause away.

    Enter OTHELLO *and* IAGO, *at a distance*

    Emil. Madam, here comes my lord.
    Cas. Madam, I 'll take my leave.   30
    Des. Nay, stay, and hear me speak.
    Cas. Madam, not now: I am very ill at ease,
Unfit for mine own purposes.
    Des. Well, do your discretion.   [*Exit Cassio.*

Iago.   Ha! I like not that.

Oth.   What dost thou say?

Iago.   Nothing, my lord: or if — I know not what.

Oth.   Was not that Cassio parted from my wife?

Iago.   Cassio, my lord! No, sure, I cannot think
it,

That he would steal away so guilty-like,

Seeing you coming.

Oth.   I do believe 't was he.   40

Des.   How now, my lord!

I have been talking with a suitor here,

A man that languishes in your displeasure.

Oth.   Who is 't you mean?

Des.   Why, your lieutenant, Cassio. Good my
lord,

If I have any grace or power to move you,

His present reconciliation take;

For if he be not one that truly loves you,

That errs in ignorance and not in cunning,

I have no judgement in an honest face;   50

I prithee, call him back.

Oth.   Went he hence now?

Des.   Ay, sooth; so humbled

That he hath left part of his grief with me,

To suffer with him. Good love, call him back.

Oth.   Not now, sweet Desdemona; some other
time.

Des.   But shall 't be shortly?

Oth.   The sooner, sweet, for you.

Des.   Shall 't be to-night at supper?

Oth.   No, not to-night.

Des.   To-morrow dinner, then?

Oth.   I shall not dine at home;
I meet the captains at the citadel.

   Des.   Why then to-morrow night; or Tuesday
     morn;   60
On Tuesday noon, or night; on Wednesday morn:
I prithee, name the time; but let it not
Exceed three days: in faith he 's penitent;
And yet his trespass, in our common reason —
Save that, they say, the wars must make examples
Out of their best — is not almost a fault
To incur a private check. When shall he come?
Tell me, Othello: I wonder in my soul,
What you would ask me, that I should deny,
Or stand so mammering on. What! Michael Cassio,   70
That came a-wooing with you, and so many a time,
When I have spoke of you dispraisingly,
Hath ta'en your part; to have so much to do
To bring him in! Trust me, I could do much, —

   Oth.   Prithee, no more: let him come when he will:
I will deny thee nothing.

   Des.   Why, this is not a boon;
'T is as I should entreat you wear your gloves,
Or feed on nourishing dishes, or keep you warm,
Or sue to you to do a peculiar profit
To your own person: nay, when I have a suit   80
Wherein I mean to touch your love indeed,
It shall be full of poise and difficult weight,
And fearful to be granted.

   Oth.   I will deny thee nothing:
Whereon, I do beseech thee, grant me this,
To leave me but a little to myself.

   Des.   Shall I deny you? no: farewell, my lord.

Oth.　Farewell, my Desdemona: I 'll come to thee
　　straight.

Des.　Emilia, come.　Be as your fancies teach you;
Whate'er you be, I am obedient.

　　　　　　　　　[*Exeunt Desdemona and Emilia.*

Oth.　Excellent wretch!　Perdition catch my soul, 90
But I do love thee! and when I love thee not,
Chaos is come again.

Iago.　My noble lord, —

Oth.　　　　　　　　What dost thou say, Iago?

Iago.　Did Michael Cassio, when you woo'd my
　　lady,
Know of your love?

Oth.　He did, from first to last: why dost thou ask?

Iago.　But for a satisfaction of my thought;
No further harm.

Oth.　　　　　　Why of thy thought, Iago?

Iago.　I did not think he had been acquainted
　　with her.

Oth.　O, yes; and went between us very oft.　100

Iago.　Indeed!

Oth.　Indeed! ay, indeed: discern'st thou aught in
　　that?
Is he not honest?

Iago.　　　　　Honest, my lord!

Oth.　　　　　　　　　　Honest! ay, honest.

Iago.　My lord, for aught I know.

Oth.　What dost thou think?

Iago.　　　　　　　　　Think, my lord!

Oth.　Think, my lord!

　　　　　　　　By heaven, he echoes me,
As if there were some monster in his thought

Too hideous to be shown. Thou dost mean some-
       thing:
I heard thee say even now, thou likedst not that,
When Cassio left my wife: what didst not like?   110
And when I told thee he was of my counsel
In my whole course of wooing, thou criedst "Indeed!"
And didst contract and purse thy brow together,
As if thou then hadst shut up in thy brain
Some horrible conceit: if thou dost love me,
Show me thy thought.

    Iago.   My lord, you know I love you.

    Oth.   I think thou dost;
And, for I know thou 'rt full of love and honesty,
And weigh'st thy words before thou givest them
       breath,
Therefore these stops of thine fright me the more: 120
For such things in a false disloyal knave
Are tricks of custom, but in a man that 's just
They are close delations, working from the heart
That passion cannot rule.

    Iago.   For Michael Cassio,
I dare be sworn I think that he is honest.

    Oth.   I think so too.

    Iago.   Men should be what they seem;
Or those that be not, would they might seem none!

    Oth.   Certain, men should be what they seem.

    Iago.   Why, then, I think Cassio's an honest man.

    Oth.   Nay, yet there 's more in this: 130
I prithee, speak to me as to thy thinkings,
As thou dost ruminate, and give thy worst of
       thoughts
The worst of words.

Iago.   Good my lord, pardon me:
Though I am bound to every act of duty,
I am not bound to that all slaves are free to.
Utter my thoughts? Why, say they are vile and
          false;
As where 's that palace whereinto foul things
Sometimes intrude not? who has a breast so pure,
But some uncleanly apprehensions
Keep leets and law-days and in session sit   14(
With meditations lawful?

Oth.   Thou dost conspire against thy friend, Iago,
If thou but think'st him wrong'd and makest his ear
A stranger to thy thoughts.

Iago.   I do beseech you —
Though I perchance am vicious in my guess,
As, I confess, it is my nature's plague
To spy into abuses, and oft my jealousy
Shapes faults that are not — that your wisdom yet,
From one that so imperfectly conceits,
Would take no notice, nor build yourself a trouble   15(
Out of his scattering and unsure observance.
It were not for your quiet nor your good,
Nor for my manhood, honesty, or wisdom,
To let you know my thoughts.

Oth.   What dost thou mean?

Iago.   Good name in man and woman, dear my
          lord,
Is the immediate jewel of their souls:
Who steals my purse steals trash; 't is something,
          nothing;
'T was mine, 't is his, and has been slave to thou-
          sands;

But he that filches from me my good name
Robs me of that which not enriches him,   160
And makes me poor indeed.

    Oth.   By heaven, I 'll know thy thoughts.

    Iago.   You cannot, if my heart were in your hand;
Nor shall not, whilst 't is in my custody.

    Oth. Ha!

    Iago.   O, beware, my lord, of jealousy;
It is the green-eyed monster which doth mock
The meat it feeds on: that cuckold lives in bliss
Who, certain of his fate, loves not his wronger;
But, O, what damned minutes tells he o'er
Who dotes, yet doubts, suspects, yet strongly loves!

    Oth. O misery!   171

    Iago.   Poor and content is rich, and rich enough,
But riches fineless is as poor as winter
To him that ever fears he shall be poor.
Good heaven, the souls of all my tribe defend
From jealousy!

    Oth.   Why, why is this?
Think'st thou I 'ld make a life of jealousy,
To follow still the changes of the moon
With fresh suspicions? No; to be once in doubt
Is once to be resolved: exchange me for a goat,   180
When I shall turn the business of my soul
To such exsufflicate and blown surmises,
Matching thy inference. 'T is not to make me
        jealous
To say my wife is fair, feeds well, loves company,
Is free of speech, sings, plays and dances well;
Where virtue is, these are more virtuous:
Nor from mine own weak merits will I draw

The smallest fear or doubt of her revolt;
For she had eyes, and chose me.   No, Iago;
I 'll see before I doubt; when I doubt, prove;   190
And on the proof, there is no more but this,
Away at once with love or jealousy!
   Iago.   I am glad of it; for now I shall have reason
To show the love and duty that I bear you
With franker spirit: therefore, as I am bound,
Receive it from me.   I speak not yet of proof.
Look to your wife; observe her well with Cassio;
Wear your eye thus, not jealous nor secure:
I would not have your free and noble nature,
Out of self-bounty, be abused; look to 't: 200
I know our country disposition well;
In Venice they do let heaven see the pranks
They dare not show their husbands; their best con-
      science
Is not to leave 't undone, but keep 't unknown.
   Oth.   Dost thou say so?
   Iago.   She did deceive her father, marrying you;
And when she seem'd to shake and fear your looks,
She loved them most.
   Oth.   <u>And so she did.</u> *climax*
   Iago.   Why, go to, then;
She that, so young, could give out such a seeming,
To seel her father's eyes up close as oak —   210
He thought 't was witchcraft; — but I am much to
      blame —
I humbly do beseech you of your pardon
For too much loving you.
   Oth.   I am bound to thee for ever.
   Iago.   I see this hath a little dash'd your spirits.

Oth. Not a jot, not a jot.

Iago.   I' faith, I fear it has.
I hope you will consider what is spoke
Comes from my love. But I do see you 're moved:
I am to pray you not to strain my speech
To grosser issues nor to larger reach
Than to suspicion.   220

Oth. I will not.

Iago.   Should you do so, my lord,
My speech should fall into such vile success
As my thoughts aim not at. Cassio 's my worthy
       friend —
My lord, I see you 're moved.

Oth.   No, not much moved:
I do not think but Desdemona 's honest.

Iago. Long live she so! and long live you to think so!

Oth. And yet, how nature erring from itself, —

Iago. Ay, there 's the point: as — to be bold
       with you —
Not to affect many proposed matches
Of her own clime, complexion, and degree,   230
Whereto we see in all things nature tends —
Foh! one may smell in such a will most rank,
Foul disproportion, thoughts unnatural.
But pardon me; I do not in position
Distinctly speak of her; though I may fear
Her will, recoiling to her better judgment,
May fall to match you with her country forms
And happily repent.

Oth.   Farewell, farewell:
If more thou dost perceive, let me know more;
Set on thy wife to observe: leave me, Iago.   240

Iago. [*Going*]   My lord, I take my leave.

Oth.   Why did I marry?   This honest creature
  doubtless

Sees and knows more, much more, than he unfolds.

Iago. [*Returning*]   My lord, I would I might entreat your honour

To scan this thing no further; leave it to time:

Though it be fit that Cassio have his place

For, sure, he fills it up with great ability,

Yet, if you please to hold him off awhile,

You shall by that perceive him and his means:

Note, if your lady strain his entertainment 250

With any strong or vehement importunity;

Much will be seen in that.   In the mean time,

Let me be thought too busy in my fears —

As worthy cause I have to fear I am —

And hold her free, I do beseech your honour.

Oth.   Fear not my government.

Iago.   I once more take my leave.   [*Exit.*

Oth.   This fellow 's of exceeding honesty,

And knows all qualities, with a learned spirit,

Of human dealings.   If I do prove her haggard, 260

Though that her jesses were my dear heart-strings,

I 'ld whistle her off and let her down the wind,

To prey at fortune.   Haply, for I am black

And have not those soft parts of conversation

That chamberers have, or for I am declined

Into the vale of years, — yet that 's not much —

She 's gone.   I am abused; and my relief

Must be to loathe her.   O curse of marriage,

That we can call these delicate creatures ours,

And not their appetites!   I had rather be a toad, 270

And live upon the vapour of a dungeon,
Than keep a corner in the thing I love
For others' uses.   Yet, 't is the plague of great ones;
Prerogatived are they less than the base;
'T is destiny unshunnable, like death:
Even then this forked plague is fated to us
When we do quicken.   Desdemona comes:

Re-enter DESDEMONA *and* EMILIA

If she be false, O, then heaven mocks itself!
I'll not believe 't.
   Des.   How now, my dear Othello!
Your dinner, and the generous islanders   280
By you invited, do attend your presence.
   Oth.   I am to blame.
   Des.   Why do you speak so faintly?
Are you not well?
   Oth.   I have a pain upon my forehead here.
   Des.   'Faith, that's with watching; 't will away
        again:
Let me but bind it hard, within this hour
It will be well.
   Oth.   Your napkin is too little:
   [*He puts the handkerchief from him; and it drops.*
Let it alone.   Come, I 'll go in with you.
   Des.   I am very sorry that you are not well.
                [*Exeunt Othello and Desdemona.*
   Emil.   I am glad I have found this napkin: 290
This was her first remembrance from the Moor:
My wayward husband hath a hundred times
Woo'd me to steal it; but she so loves the token,
For he conjured her she should ever keep it,

That she reserves it evermore about her
To kiss and talk to.   I 'll have the work ta'en out,
And give 't Iago: what he will do with it
Heaven knows, not I;
I nothing but to please his fantasy.

Re-enter Iago

   Iago.   How now! what do you here alone?   300
   Emil.   Do not you chide; I have a thing for
     you.
   Iago.   A thing for me? it is a common thing —
   Emil.   Ha!
   Iago.   To have a foolish wife.
   Emil.   O, is that all?   What will you give me
     now
For that same handkerchief?
   Iago.   What handkerchief?
   Emil.   What handkerchief!
Why, that the Moor first gave to Desdemona;
That which so often you did bid me steal.
   Iago.   Hast stol'n it from her?   310
   Emil.   No, 'faith; she let it drop by negligence,
And, to the advantage, I, being here, took 't up.
Look, here it is.
   Iago.   A good wench; give it me.
   Emil.   What will you do with 't, that you have
     been so earnest
To have me filch it?
   Iago.   [*Snatching it*]   Why, what 's that to you?
   Emil.   If 't be not for some purpose of import
Give 't me again: poor lady, she 'll run mad
When she shall lack it.

Iago.   Be not acknown on 't; I have use for it.
Go, leave me.   [*Exit Emilia.* 320
I will in Cassio's lodging lose this napkin,
And let him find it.   Trifles light as air
Are to the jealous confirmations strong
As proofs of holy writ: this may do something.
The Moor already changes with my poison:
Dangerous conceits are in their natures poisons,
Which at the first are scarce found to distaste,
But with a little act upon the blood,
Burn like the mines of sulphur.   I did say so:
Look, where he comes!

Re-enter OTHELLO

                         Not poppy, nor mandragora,   330
Nor all the drowsy syrups of the world,
Shall ever medicine thee to that sweet sleep
Which thou owedst yesterday.
    Oth.   Ha! ha! false to me?
    Iago.   Why, how now, general! no more of that.
    Oth.   Avaunt! be gone! thou hast set me on the
          rack:
I swear 't is better to be much abused
Than but to know 't a little.
    Iago.   How now, my lord!
    Oth.   What sense had I of her stol'n hours of lust?
I saw 't not, thought it not, it harm'd not me:
I slept the next night well, was free and merry;   340
I found not Cassio's kisses on her lips:
He that is robb'd, not wanting what is stol'n,
Let him not know 't, and he 's not robb'd at all.
    Iago.   I am sorry to hear this.

   Oth. I had been happy, if the general camp,
Pioners and all, had tasted her sweet body,
So I had nothing known. O, now for ever
Farewell the tranquil mind! farewell content!
Farewell the plumed troop and the big wars
That make ambition virtue! O, farewell!   350
Farewell the neighing steed and the shrill trump,
The spirit-stirring drum, the ear-piercing fife,
The royal banner, and all quality,
Pride, pomp and circumstance of glorious war!
And, O you mortal engines, whose rude throats
The immortal Jove's dread clamours counterfeit,
Farewell!   Othello's occupation 's gone!
   Iago. Is 't possible, my lord?
   Oth. Villain, be sure thou prove my love a whore,
Be sure of it; give me the ocular proof;   360
Or, by the worth of man's eternal soul,
Thou hadst been better have been born a dog
Than answer my waked wrath!
   Iago.   Is 't come to this?
   Oth. Make me to see 't; at the least, so prove it,
That the probation bear no hinge nor loop
To hang a doubt on; or woe upon thy life!
   Iago. My noble lord, —
   Oth. If thou dost slander her and torture me,
Never pray more; abandon all remorse;
On horror's head horrors accumulate;   370
Do deeds to make heaven weep, all earth amazed;
For nothing canst thou to damnation add
Greater than that.
   Iago.   O grace! O heaven forgive me!
Are you a man? have you a soul or sense?

God be wi' you; take mine office. O wretched fool,
That livest to make thine honesty a vice!
O monstrous world! Take note, take note, O world,
To be direct and honest is not safe.
I thank you for this profit, and from hence
I 'll love no friend, sith love breeds such offence.   380
   Oth. Nay, stay: thou shouldst be honest.
   Iago. I should be wise, for honesty 's a fool
And loses that it works for.
   Oth.   By the world,
I think my wife be honest, and think she is not;
I think that thou art just, and think thou art not.
I 'll have some proof. Her name, that was as fresh
As Dian's visage, is now begrimed and black
As mine own face. If there be cords, or knives,
Poison, or fire, or suffocating streams,
I 'll not endure it. Would I were satisfied!   390
   Iago. I see, sir, you are eaten up with passion:
I do repent me that I put it to you.
You would be satisfied?
   Oth.   Would! nay, I will.
   Iago. And may: but, how? how satisfied, my
        lord?
Would you, the supervisor, grossly gape on —
Behold her topp'd?
   Oth.   Death and damnation! O!
   Iago. It were a tedious difficulty I think,
To bring them to that prospect: damn them then,
If ever mortal eyes do see them bolster
More than their own! What then? how then?   400
What shall I say? Where 's satisfaction?
It is impossible you should see this,

Were they as prime as goats, as hot as monkeys,
As salt as wolves in pride, and fools as gross
As ignorance made drunk.   But yet, I say,
If imputation and strong circumstances,
Which lead directly to the door of truth,
Will give you satisfaction, you may have 't.

   Oth.   Give me a living reason she 's disloyal.

   Iago.   I do not like the office: 410
But, sith I am enter'd in this cause so far,
Prick'd to 't by foolish honesty and love,
I will go on.   I lay with Cassio lately;
And, being troubled with a raging tooth,
I could not sleep.
There are a kind of men so loose of soul,
That in their sleeps will mutter their affairs:
One of this kind is Cassio:
In sleep I heard him say "Sweet Desdemona,
Let us be wary, let us hide our loves";   420
And then, sir, would he gripe and wring my hand,
Cry "O sweet creature!" and then kiss me hard,
As if he pluck'd up kisses by the roots,
That grew upon my lips: then sigh'd, and then
Cried "Cursed fate that gave thee to the Moor!"

   Oth.   O monstrous! monstrous!

   Iago.   Nay, this was but his dream.

   Oth.   But this denoted a foregone conclusion:
'T is a shrewd doubt, though it be but a dream.

   Iago.   And this may help to thicken other proofs 430
That do demonstrate thinly.

   Oth.   I 'll tear her all to pieces.

   Iago.   Nay, but be wise: yet we see nothing done;
She may be honest yet.   Tell me but this,

Have you not sometimes seen a handkerchief
Spotted with strawberries in your wife's hand?

 Oth. I gave her such a one; 't was my first gift.

 Iago. I know not that: but such a handkerchief —
I am sure it was your wife's — did I to-day
See Cassio wipe his beard with.

 Oth.   If it be that, —

 Iago. If it be that, or any that was hers,   440
It speaks against her with the other proofs.

 Oth. O, that the slave had forty thousand lives!
One is too poor, too weak for my revenge.
Now do I see 't is true. Look here, Iago;
All my fond love thus do I blow to heaven.
'T is gone.
Arise, black vengeance, from thy hollow cell!
Yield up, O love, thy crown and hearted throne
To tyrannous hate! Swell, bosom, with thy fraught,
For 't is of aspics' tongues!

 Iago.   Yet be content.   450

 Oth. O, blood, blood, blood!

 Iago. Patience, I say; your mind perhaps may
    change.

 Oth. Never, Iago. Like to the Pontic sea,
Whose icy current and compulsive course
Ne'er feels retiring ebb, but keeps due on
To the Propontic and the Hellespont,
Even so my bloody thoughts, with violent pace,
Shall ne'er look back, ne'er ebb to humble love,
Till that a capable and wide revenge
Swallow them up. Now, by yond marble heaven, 460
[*Kneels*] In the due reverence of a sacred vow
I here engage my words.

Iago.   Do not rise yet.
[*Kneels*]   Witness, you ever-burning lights above,
You elements that clip us round about,
Witness that here Iago doth give up
The execution of his wit, hands, heart,
To wrong'd Othello's service!   Let him command,
And to obey shall be in me remorse,
What bloody business ever.   [*They rise.*

   Oth.   I greet thy love,
Not with vain thanks, but with acceptance bounte-
          ous,
And will upon the instant put thee to 't: 471
Within these three days let me hear thee say
That Cassio 's not alive.

   Iago.   My friend is dead; 't is done at your
          request:
But let her live.

   Oth.   Damn her, lewd minx! O, damn
          her!
Come, go with me apart; I will withdraw,
To furnish me with some swift means of death
For the fair devil.   Now art thou my lieutenant.

   Iago.   I am your own for ever.   [*Exeunt.*

Scene IV — *Before the castle*

Enter Desdemona, Emilia, *and* Clown

   Des.   Do you know, sirrah, where Lieutenant
Cassio lies?

   Clo.   I dare not say he lies any where.

   Des.   Why, man?

   Clo.   He is a soldier, and for one to say a soldier
lies, is stabbing.

Des. Go to: where lodges he?

Clo. To tell you where he lodges, is to tell you where I lie.

Des. Can any thing be made of this? 10

Clo. I know not where he lodges, and for me to devise a lodging and say he lies here or he lies there, were to lie in mine own throat.

Des. Can you inquire him out, and be edified by report?

Clo. I will catechize the world for him; that is, make questions, and by them answer.

Des. Seek him, bid him come hither: tell him I have moved my lord on his behalf, and hope all will be well. 20

Clo. To do this is within the compass of man's wit; and therefore I will attempt the doing it. [*Exit.*

Des. Where should I lose that handkerchief, Emilia?

Emil. I know not, madam.

Des. Believe me, I had rather have lost my purse
Full of crusadoes: and, but my noble Moor
Is true of mind and made of no such baseness
As jealous creatures are, it were enough
To put him to ill thinking.

Emil. Is he not jealous? 29

Des. Who, he? I think the sun where he was born
Drew all such humours from him.

Emil. Look, where he comes.

Des. I will not leave him now till Cassio
Be call'd to him.

Enter OTHELLO

     How is 't with you, my lord?
 Oth. Well, my good lady. [*Aside*] O, hardness
    to dissemble! —
How do you, Desdemona?
 Des.   Well, my good lord.
 Oth. Give me your hand: this hand is moist,
    my lady.
 Des. It yet hath felt no age nor known no sorrow.
 Oth. This argues fruitfulness and liberal heart:
Hot, hot, and moist: this hand of yours requires
A sequester from liberty, fasting and prayer,   40
Much castigation, exercise devout;
For here 's a young and sweating devil here,
That commonly rebels.   'T is a good hand,
A frank one.
 Des. You may, indeed, say so;
For 't was that hand that gave away my heart.
 Oth. A liberal hand: the hearts of old gave hands;
But our new heraldry is hands, not hearts.
 Des. I cannot speak of this.   Come now, your
    promise.
 Oth. What promise, chuck?   49
 Des. I have sent to bid Cassio come speak with
    you.
 Oth. I have a salt and sorry rheum offends me;
Lend me thy handkerchief.
 Des.   Here, my lord.
 Oth. That which I gave you.
 Des.   I have it not about me.
 Oth. Not?

Des.   No, indeed, my lord.

Oth.   That 's a fault.   That handkerchief
Did an Egyptian to my mother give;
She was a charmer, and could almost read
The thoughts of people: she told her, while she kept it,
'T would make her amiable and subdue my father
Entirely to her love, but if she lost it   60
Or made a gift of it, my father's eye
Should hold her loathed and his spirits should hunt
After new fancies: she, dying, gave it me;
And bid me, when my fate would have me wive,
To give it her.   I did so: and take heed on 't;
Make it a darling like your precious eye;
To lose 't or give 't away were such perdition
As nothing else could match.

Des.   Is 't possible?

Oth.   'T is true: there 's magic in the web of it
A sibyl, that had number'd in the world   70
The sun to course two hundred compasses,
In her prophetic fury sew'd the work;
The worms were hallow'd that did breed the silk;
And it was dyed in mummy which the skilful
Conserved of maidens' hearts.

Des.   Indeed! is 't true?

Oth.   Most veritable; therefore look to 't well.

Des.   Then would to God that I had never seen 't!

Oth.   Ha! wherefore?

Des.   Why do you speak so startingly and rash?   79

Oth.   Is 't lost? is 't gone? speak, is it out o' the
          way?

Des.   Heaven bless us!

Oth.   Say you?

   Des. It is not lost; but what an if it were?

   Oth. How!

   Des. I say, it is not lost.

   Oth.   Fetch 't, let me see 't.

   Des. Why, so I can, sir, but I will not now.
This is a trick to put me from my suit:
Pray you, let Cassio be received again.

   Oth. Fetch me the handkerchief: my mind mis-
       gives.

   Des. Come, come;   90
You 'll never meet a more sufficient man.

   Oth. The handkerchief!

   Des.   I pray, talk me of Cassio.

   Oth. The handkerchief!

   Des.   A man that all his time
Hath founded his good fortunes on your love,
Shared dangers with you, —

   Oth. The handkerchief!

   Des. In sooth, you are to blame.

   Oth. Away!   [*Exit.*

   Emil. Is not this man jealous?

   Des. I ne'er saw this before.   100
Sure, there's some wonder in this handkerchief:
I am most unhappy in the loss of it.

   Emil. 'T is not a year or two shows us a man:
They are all but stomachs, and we all but food;
They eat us hungerly, and when they are full,
They belch us. Look you, Cassio and my husband!

Enter Cassio *and* Iago

   Iago. There is no other way; 't is she must do 't:
And, lo, the happiness! go, and importune her.

Des.   How now, good Cassio! what's the news
        with you?

Cas.   Madam, my former suit: I do beseech 110
        you

That by your virtuous means I may again

Exist, and be a member of his love

Whom I with all the office of my heart

Entirely honour: I would not be delay'd.

If my offence be of such mortal kind

That nor my service past, nor present sorrows,

Nor purposed merit in futurity,

Can ransom me into his love again,

But to know so must be my benefit;

So shall I clothe me in a forced content,   120

And shut myself up in some other course,

To fortune's alms.

Des.   Alas, thrice-gentle Cassio!

My advocation is not now in tune;

My lord is not my lord; nor should I know him

Were he in favour as in humour alter'd.

So help me every spirit sanctified,

As I have spoken for you all my best

And stood within the blank of his displeasure

For my free speech! you must awhile be patient:

What I can do I will; and more I will   130

Than for myself I dare: let that suffice you.

Iago.   Is my lord angry?

Emil.   He went hence but now,

And certainly in strange unquietness.

Iago.   Can he be angry? I have seen the cannon,

When it hath blown his ranks into the air,

And, like the devil, from his very arm

Puff'd his own brother: — and can he be angry?
Something of moment then: I will go meet him:
There 's matter in 't indeed, if he be angry.

   Des. I prithee, do so.   [*Exit Iago.*
                   Something, sure, of state, 140
Either from Venice, or some unhatch'd practice
Made demonstrable here in Cyprus to him,
Hath puddled his clear spirit; and in such cases
Men's natures wrangle with inferior things,
Though great ones are their object.   'T is even so;
For let our finger ache, and it indues
Our other healthful members even to that sense
Of pain: nay, we must think men are not gods,
Nor of them look for such observances
As fit the bridal.   Beshrew me much, Emilia,   150
I was, unhandsome warrior as I am,
Arraigning his unkindness with my soul;
But now I find I had suborn'd the witness,
And he 's indicted falsely.

   Emil. Pray heaven it be state-matters, as you
        think,
And no conception nor no jealous toy
Concerning you.

   Des. Alas the day, I never gave him cause!

   Emil. But jealous souls will not be answer'd so;
They are not ever jealous for the cause,   160
But jealous for they are jealous: 't is a monster
Begot upon itself, born on itself.

   Des. Heaven keep that monster from Othello's
        mind!

   Emil. Lady, amen.

   Des. I will go seek him. Cassio, walk hereabout:

If I do find him fit, I 'll move your suit,
And seek to effect it to my uttermost.

   Cas.   I humbly thank your ladyship.

                  [Exeunt Desdemona and Emilia.

Enter BIANCA

   Bian.   Save you, friend Cassio!

   Cas.   What make you from home?
How is it with you, my most fair Bianca?   170
I' faith, sweet love, I was coming to your house.

   Bian.   And I was going to your lodging, Cassio.
What, keep a week away? seven days and nights?
Eight score eight hours? and lovers' absent hours,
More tedious than the dial eight score times?
O weary reckoning!

   Cas.   Pardon me, Bianca:
I have this while with leaden thoughts been press'd;
But I shall, in a more continuate time,
Strike off this score of absence.   Sweet Bianca,

          [Giving her Desdemona's handkerchief.
Take me this work out.

   Bian.   O Cassio, whence came this? 180
This is some token from a newer friend:
To the felt absence now I feel a cause:

       now
Is 't come to this?   Well, well.

   Cas.   Go to, woman!
Throw your vile guesses in the devil's teeth,
From whence you have them. You are jealous
That this is from some mistress, some remembrance:
No, in good troth, Bianca.

   Bian.   Why, whose is it?

Cas. I know not, sweet: I found it in my
  chamber.
I like the work well: ere it be demanded —
As like enough it will — I 'ld have it copied: 190
Take it, and do 't; and leave me for this time.
 Bian. Leave you! wherefore?
 Cas. I do attend here on the general;
And think it no addition, nor my wish,
To have him see me woman'd.
 Bian.   Why, I pray you?
 Cas. Not that I love you not.
 Bian.   But that you do not love me.
I pray you, bring me on the way a little,
And say if I shall see you soon at night.
 Cas. 'Tis but a little way that I can bring you;
For I attend here: but I 'll see you soon. 200
 Bian. 'T is very good; I must be circumstanced.
         [*Exeunt.*

ACT IV

Scene I — *Cyprus.   Before the castle*

Enter Othello *and* Iago

 Iago. Will you think so?
 Oth.   Think so, Iago!
 Iago.   What,
To kiss in private?
 Oth.   An unauthorized kiss.
 Iago. Or to be naked with her friend in bed
An hour or more, not meaning any harm?
 Oth. Naked in bed, Iago, and not mean harm!

It is hypocrisy against the devil:
They that mean virtuously, and yet do so,
The devil their virtue tempts, and they tempt
       heaven.

    Iago. So they do nothing, 't is a venial slip;
But if I give my wife a handkerchief, —   10

    Oth. What then?

    Iago. Why, then, 't is hers, my lord; and, being
       hers,
She may, I think, bestow 't on any man.

    Oth. She is protectress of her honour too:
May she give that?

    Iago. Her honour is an essence that 's not seen;
They have it very oft that have it not:
But, for the handkerchief, —

    Oth. By heaven, I would most gladly have for-
       got it.
Thou said'st — O, it comes o'er my memory   20
As doth the raven o'er the infected house,
Boding to all — he had my handkerchief.

    Iago. Ay, what of that?

    Oth.   That 's not so good now.

    Iago.   What,
If I had said I had seen him do you wrong?
Or heard him say, — as knaves be such abroad,
Who having, by their own importunate suit,
Or voluntary dotage of some mistress,
Convinced or supplied them, cannot choose
But they must blab—

    Oth.   Hath he said any thing?

    Iago. He hath, my lord; but be you well assured, 30
No more than he 'll unswear.

Oth.   What hath he said?

Iago.   'Faith, that he did — I know not what he did.

Oth.   What? what?

Iago.   Lie —

Oth.   With her?

Iago.   With her, on her; what you will.

Oth.   Lie with her! lie on her! We say lie on her, when they belie her. Lie with her! that 's fulsome. — Handkerchief — confessions — handkerchief! — To confess, and be hanged for his labour; — first to be hanged, and then to confess. — I tremble at it. Nature would not invest herself in such shadowing passion without some instruction. It is not words that shake me thus. Pish! Noses, ears, and lips. — Is 't possible? — Confess — handkerchief! — O devil!

                   [*Falls in a trance.*

Iago.   Work on,
My medicine, work! Thus credulous fools are caught;
And many worthy and chaste dames even thus,
All guiltless, meet reproach. What, ho! my lord!
My lord, I say! Othello!

Enter Cassio

            How now, Cassio!

Cas.   What 's the matter?   50

Iago.   My lord is fall'n into an epilepsy:
This is his second fit; he had one yesterday.

Cas.   Rub him about the temples.

Iago.   No, forbear;
The lethargy must have his quiet course:

If not, he foams at mouth and by and by
Breaks out to savage madness. Look, he stirs:
Do you withdraw yourself a little while,
He will recover straight: when he is gone,
I would on great occasion speak with you.

[Exit Cassio.

How is it, general? have you not hurt your head?   60
   Oth.   Dost thou mock me?
   Iago.   I mock you! no, by heaven.
Would you would bear your fortune like a man!
   Oth.   A horned man 's a monster and a beast.
   Iago.   There 's many a beast then in a populous
        city,
And many a civil monster.
   Oth.   Did he confess it?
   Iago.   Good sir, be a man;
Think every bearded fellow that 's but yoked
May draw with you: there's millions now alive
That nightly lie in those unproper beds
Which they dare swear peculiar: your case is better.   70
O, 't is the spite of hell, the fiend's arch-mock,
To lip a wanton in a secure couch,
And to suppose her chaste! No, let me know;
And knowing what I am, I know what she shall be.
   Oth.   O, thou art wise; 't is certain.
   Iago.   Stand you awhile apart;
Confine yourself but in a patient list.
Whilst you were here o'erwhelmed with your grief —
A passion most unsuiting such a man —
Cassio came hither: I shifted him away,
And laid good 'scuse upon your ecstasy,   80
Bade him anon return and here speak with me;

The which he promised.   Do but encave yourself,
And mark the fleers, the gibes, and notable scorns,
That dwell in every region of his face;
For I will make him tell the tale anew,
Where, how, how oft, how long ago, and when
He hath, and is again to cope your wife:
I say, but mark his gesture.   Marry, patience;
Or I shall say you are all in all in spleen,
And nothing of a man.

   Oth.   Dost thou hear, Iago?   9c
I will be found most cunning in my patience;
But — dost thou hear? — most bloody.

   Iago.   That 's not amiss;
But yet keep time in all.   Will you withdraw?

                            [Othello retires.

Now will I question Cassio of Bianca,
A housewife that by selling her desires
Buys herself bread and clothes: it is a creature
That dotes on Cassio; as 't is the strumpet's plague
To beguile many and be beguiled by one:
He, when he hears of her, cannot refrain
From the excess of laughter.   Here he comes: 10c

Re-enter CASSIO

As he shall smile, Othello shall go mad;
And his unbookish jealousy must construe
Poor Cassio's smiles, gestures and light behaviour,
Quite in the wrong.   How do you now, lieutenant?

   Cas.   The worser that you give me the addition
Whose want even kills me.

   Iago.   Ply Desdemona well, and you are sure
      on 't.

[*Speaking lower*]   Now, if this suit lay in Bianca's
      power,
How quickly should you speed!

  Cas.   Alas, poor caitiff!

  Oth.   Look, how he laughs already!   110

  Iago.   I never knew woman love man so.

  Cas.   Alas, poor rogue! I think, i' faith, she loves
      me.

  Oth.   Now he denies it faintly, and laughs it out.

  Iago.   Do you hear, Cassio?

  Oth.   Now he importunes him
To tell it o'er: go to; well said, well said.

  Iago.   She gives it out that you shall marry her:
Do you intend it?

  Cas.   Ha, ha, ha!   120

  Oth.   Do you triumph, Roman? do you triumph?

  Cas.   I marry her! what? a customer! Prithee,
bear some charity to my wit; do not think it so
unwholesome. Ha, ha, ha!

  Oth.   So, so, so, so: they laugh that win.

  Iago.   'Faith, the cry goes that you shall marry
      her.

  Cas.   Prithee, say true.

  Iago.   I am a very villain else.

  Oth.   Have you scored me? Well.   130

  Cas.   This is the monkey's own giving out: she is
persuaded I will marry her, out of her own love and
flattery, not out of my promise.

  Oth.   Iago beckons me; now he begins the story.

  Cas.   She was here even now; she haunts me in
every place. I was the other day talking on the
sea-bank with certain Venetians; and thither comes

the bauble, and, by this hand, she falls me thus
about my neck —   140

Oth. Crying "O dear Cassio!" as it were: his
gesture imports it.

Cas. So hangs, and lolls, and weeps upon me;
so hales, and pulls me: ha, ha, ha!

Oth. Now he tells how she plucked him to my
chamber. O, I see that nose of yours, but not that
dog I shall throw it to.

Cas. Well, I must leave her company.

Iago. Before me! look, where she comes.

Cas. 'T is such another fitchew! marry, a per-
fumed one.

Enter BIANCA

What do you mean by this haunting of me?

Bian. Let the devil and his dam haunt you!
What did you mean by that same handkerchief you
gave me even now? I was a fine fool to take it.
I must take out the work? — A likely piece of work,
that you should find it in your chamber, and not
know who left it there! This is some minx's token,
and I must take out the work? There; give it your
hobby-horse: wheresoever you had it, I 'll take out
no work on 't.   161

Cas. How now, my sweet Bianca! how now!
how now!

Oth. By heaven, that should be my handkerchief!

Bian. An you 'll come to supper to-night, you
may; an you will not, come when you are next
prepared for.   [*Exit.*

Iago. After her, after her.   170

Cas. 'Faith, I must; she 'll rail in the street else.

Iago. Will you sup there?

Cas. 'Faith, I intend so.

Iago. Well, I may chance to see you: for I would very fain speak with you.

Cas. Prithee, come; will you?

Iago. Go to; say no more. [*Exit Cassio.*

Oth. [*Advancing*] How shall I murder him, Iago? 180

Iago. Did you perceive how he laughed at his vice?

Oth. O Iago!

Iago. And did you see the handkerchief?

Oth. Was that mine?

Iago. Yours, by this hand: and to see how he prizes the foolish woman your wife! she gave it him, and he hath given it his whore.

Oth. I would have him nine years a-killing. A fine woman! a fair woman! a sweet woman!

Iago. Nay, you must forget that. 190

Oth. Ay, let her rot, and perish, and be damned to-night; for she shall not live: no, my heart is turned to stone; I strike it, and it hurts my hand. O, the world hath not a sweeter creature: she might lie by an emperor's side and command him tasks.

Iago. Nay, that's not your way.

Oth. Hang her! I do but say what she is: so delicate with her needle: an admirable musician: O! she will sing the savageness out of a bear: of so high and plenteous wit and invention:— 201

Iago. She's the worse for all this.

Oth. O, a thousand thousand times: and then, of so gentle a condition!

Iago. Ay, too gentle.

Oth.   Nay, that 's certain: but yet the pity of it, Iago! O Iago, the pity of it, Iago!

Iago.   If you are so fond over her iniquity, give her patent to offend; for, if it touch not you, it comes near nobody.   210

Oth.   I will chop her into messes: cuckold me!

Iago.   O, 't is foul in her.

Oth.   With mine officer!

Iago.   That 's fouler.

Oth.   Get me some poison, Iago; this night: I 'll not expostulate with her, lest her body and beauty unprovide my mind again: this night, Iago.   219

Iago.   Do it not with poison, strangle her in her bed, even the bed she hath contaminated.

Oth.   Good, good: the justice of it pleases: very good.

Iago.   And for Cassio, let me be his undertaker: you shall hear more by midnight.

Oth.   Excellent good. [*A trumpet within.*] What trumpet is that same?

Iago.   Something from Venice, sure. 'T is Lodovico Come from the duke: and, see, your wife is with him.

Enter LODOVICO, DESDEMONA, *and* Attendants

Lod.   Save you, worthy general!

Oth.   With all my heart, sir.

Lod.   The duke and senators of Venice greet you.
                          [*Gives him a letter.*

Oth.   I kiss the instrument of their pleasures.   230
                          [*Opens the letter, and reads.*

Des. And what's the news, good cousin Lodovico?

Iago. I am very glad to see you, signior;
Welcome to Cyprus.

Lod. I thank you. How does Lieutenant Cassio?

Iago. Lives, sir.

Des. Cousin, there's fall'n between him and my
    lord
An unkind breach: but you shall make all well.

Oth. Are you sure of that?

Des. My lord?

Oth. [*Reads*] "This fail you not to do, as you
    will —"

Lod. He did not call; he's busy in the paper. 241
Is there division 'twixt my lord and Cassio?

Des. A most unhappy one: I would do much
To atone them, for the love I bear to Cassio.

Oth. Fire and brimstone!

Des.   My lord?

Oth.   Are you wise?

Des. What, is he angry?

Lod.   May be the letter moved him;
For, as I think, they do command him home,
Deputing Cassio in his government.

Des. Trust me, I am glad on 't.

Oth.   Indeed!

Des.   My lord?

Oth. I am glad to see you mad.

Des.   Why, sweet Othello, —

Oth. [*Striking her*] Devil! 251

Des. I have not deserved this.

Lod. My lord, this would not be believed in
    Venice,

Though I should swear I saw 't: 't is very much:
Make her amends; she weeps.

   Oth.   O devil, devil!
If that the earth could teem with woman's tears,
Each drop she falls would prove a crocodile.
Out of my sight!

   Des.   I will not stay to offend you.   [*Going.*

   Lod.   Truly, an obedient lady:
I do beseech your lordship, call her back.   260

   Oth.   Mistress!

   Des.   My lord?

   Oth.   What would you with her, sir?

   Lod.   Who, I, my lord?

   Oth.   Ay; you did wish that I would make her
       turn:
Sir, she can turn, and turn, and yet go on,
And turn again; and she can weep, sir, weep;
And she 's obedient, as you say, obedient,
Very obedient. Proceed you in your tears,
Concerning this, sir, — O well-painted passion! —
I am commanded home. Get away you;
I 'll send for you anon. Sir, I obey the mandate,   270
And will return to Venice. Hence, avaunt!

                           [*Exit Desdemona.*

Cassio shall have my place. And, sir, to-night,
I do entreat that we may sup together:
You are welcome, sir, to Cyprus. — Goats and
       monkeys!   [*Exit.*

   Lod.   Is this the noble Moor whom our full senate
Call all in all sufficient? Is this the nature
Whom passion could not shake? whose solid virtue
The shot of accident, nor dart of chance,

Could neither graze nor pierce?

    Iago.   He is much changed.

    Lod.   Are his wits safe? is he not light of brain?   280

    Iago.   He 's that he is: I may not breathe my
           censure

What he might be: if what he might he is not,

I would to heaven he were!

    Lod.   What, strike his wife!

    Iago.   'Faith, that was not so well; yet would I
           knew

That stroke would prove the worst!

    Lod.   Is it his use?

Or did the letters work upon his blood,

And new-create his fault?

    Iago.   Alas, alas!

It is not honesty in me to speak

What I have seen and known. You shall observe
         him,

And his own courses will denote him so   290

That I may save my speech: do but go after,

And mark how he continues.

    Lod.   I am sorry that I am deceived in him.

                           [Exeunt.

SCENE II — *A room in the castle*

Enter OTHELLO *and* EMILIA

    Oth.   You have seen nothing then?

    Emil.   Nor ever heard, nor ever did suspect.

    Oth.   Yes, you have seen Cassio and she together.

    Emil.   But then I saw no harm, and then I heard

Each syllable that breath made up between them.

    Oth.   What, did they never whisper?

Emil.   Never, my lord. 10

Oth.   Nor send you out o' the way?

Emil.   Never.

Oth.   To fetch her fan, her gloves, her mask, nor
        nothing?

Emil.   Never, my lord.

Oth.   That 's strange.

Emil.   I durst, my lord, to wager she is honest,
Lay down my soul at stake: if you think other,
Remove your thought; it doth abuse your bosom.
If any wretch have put this in your head,
Let heaven requite it with the serpent's curse!
For, if she be not honest, chaste, and true,
There 's no man happy; the purest of their wives
Is foul as slander.

Oth.   Bid her come hither: go.

                                [Exit Emilia.

She says enough; yet she 's a simple bawd   20
That cannot say as much. This is a subtle whore,
A closet lock and key of villanous secrets:
And yet she 'll kneel and pray; I have seen her do 't.

Enter Desdemona *with* Emilia

Des.   My lord, what is your will?

Oth.   Pray, chuck, come hither.

Des.   What is your pleasure?

Oth.   Let me see your eyes;
Look in my face.

Des.   What horrible fancy 's this?

Oth.   [*To Emilia*] Some of your function, mistress;
Leave procreants alone and shut the door;
Cough, or cry "hem," if any body come:

Your mystery, your mystery: nay, dispatch.   30
                    [*Exit Emilia.*

   Des. Upon my knees, what doth your speech
      import?
I understand a fury in your words,
But not the words.
   Oth. Why, what art thou?
   Des.   Your wife, my lord; your true
And loyal wife.
   Oth.   Come, swear it, damn thyself;
Lest, being like one of heaven, the devils themselves
Should fear to seize thee: therefore be double damn'd;
Swear thou art honest.
   Des.   Heaven doth truly know it.
   Oth. Heaven truly knows that thou art false as
      hell.
   Des. To whom, my lord? with whom? how am I
      false?   40
   Oth. O Desdemona! Away! away! away!
   Des. Alas the heavy day! Why do you weep?
Am I the motive of these tears, my lord?
If haply you my father do suspect
An instrument of this your calling back,
Lay not your blame on me: if you have lost him,
Why, I have lost him too.
   Oth.   Had it pleased heaven
To try me with affliction; had they rain'd
All kinds of sores and shames on my bare head,
Steep'd me in poverty to the very lips,   50
Given to captivity me and my utmost hopes,
I should have found in some place of my soul
A drop of patience: but, alas, to make me

A fixed figure for the time of scorn
To point his slow unmoving finger at!
Yet could I bear that too; well, very well:
But there, where I have garner'd up my heart,
Where either I must live, or bear no life;
The fountain from the which my current runs,
Or else dries up; to be discarded thence!   60
Or keep it as a cistern for foul toads
To knot and gender in! Turn thy complexion there,
Patience, thou young and rose-lipp'd cherubin, —
Ay, there, look grim as hell!

    Des. I hope my noble lord esteems me honest.

    Oth. O, ay; as summer flies are in the shambles,
That quicken even with blowing. O thou weed,
Who art so lovely fair and smell'st so sweet
That the sense aches at thee, would thou hadst ne'er
        been born!

    Des. Alas, what ignorant sin have I committed?

    Oth. Was this fair paper, this most goodly book,
Made to write "whore" upon? What committed! 70
Committed! O thou public commoner!
I should make very forges of my cheeks,
That would to cinders burn up modesty,
Did I but speak thy deeds. What committed!
Heaven stops the nose at it and the moon winks,
The bawdy wind that kisses all it meets
Is hush'd within the hollow mine of earth,
And will not hear it. What committed!   80
Impudent strumpet!

    Des.   By heaven, you do me wrong.

    Oth. Are you not a strumpet?

    Des.   No, as I am a Christian:

If to preserve this vessel for my lord
From any other foul unlawful touch
Be not to be a strumpet, I am none.

   Oth. What, not a whore?

   Des.   No, as I shall be saved.

   Oth. Is 't possible?

   Des. O, heaven forgive us!

   Oth.   I cry you mercy, then:
I took you for that cunning whore of Venice
That married with Othello.   [*Raising his voice.*

    You, mistress,   90
That have the office opposite to Saint Peter,
And keep the gate of hell!

Re-enter Emilia

                You, you, ay, you!
We have done our course; there 's money for your
     pains:
I pray you, turn the key and keep our counsel.
                            [*Exit.*

   Emil. Alas, what does this gentleman conceive?
How do you, madam? how do you, my good
     lady?

   Des. 'Faith, half asleep.

   Emil. Good madam, what 's the matter with my
     lord?

   Des. With who?

   Emil. Why, with my lord, madam.   100

   Des. Who is thy lord?

   Emil.   He that is yours, sweet lady.

   Des. I have none: do not talk to me, Emilia;
I cannot weep; nor answer have I none,

But what should go by water.   Prithee, to-night
Lay on my bed my wedding sheets: remember;
And call thy husband hither.

    Emil.   Here 's a change indeed!   [*Exit.*

    Des.   'T is meet I should be used so, very meet.
How have I been behaved, that he might stick
The small'st opinion on my least misuse?

Re-enter Emilia with Iago

    Iago.   What is your pleasure, madam?   How is 't
        with you!   110

    Des.   I cannot tell.   Those that do teach young
        babes
Do it with gentle means and easy tasks:
He might have chid me so; for, in good faith,
I am a child to chiding.

    Iago.   What 's the matter, lady?

    Emil.   Alas, Iago, my lord hath so bewhored her,
Thrown such despite and heavy terms upon her,
As true hearts cannot bear.

    Des.   Am I that name, Iago?

    Iago.   What name, fair lady?

    Des.   Such as she says my lord did say I was.

    Emil.   He call'd her whore: a beggar in his drink 120
Could not have laid such terms upon his callet.

    Iago.   Why did he so?

    Des.   I do not know; I am sure I am none such.

    Iago.   Do not weep, do not weep.   Alas the day!

    Emil.   Hath she forsook so many noble matches,
Her father and her country and her friends,
To be call'd whore? would it not make one weep?

    Des.   It is my wretched fortune.

Iago.   Beshrew him for 't!
How comes this trick upon him?

    Des.   Nay, heaven doth know.

    Emil. I will be hang'd, if some eternal villain,   130
Some busy and insinuating rogue,
Some cogging, cozening slave, to get some office,
Have not devised this slander; I 'll be hang'd else.

    Iago. Fie, there is no such man; it is impossible.

    Des. If any such there be, heaven pardon him!

    Emil. A halter pardon him! and hell gnaw his
        bones!
Why should he call her whore? who keeps her com-
        pany?
What place? what time? what form? what likelihood?
The Moor abused by some most villanous knave,
Some base notorious knave, some scurvy fellow.   140
O heaven, that such companions thou 'ldst unfold,
And put in every honest hand a whip
To lash the rascals naked through the world
Even from the east to the west!

    Iago.   Speak within door.

    Emil. O, fie upon them! Some such squire he
        was
That turn'd your wit the seamy side without,
And made you to suspect me with the Moor.

    Iago. You are a fool; go to.

    Des.   O good Iago,
What shall I do to win my lord again?
Good friend, go to him; for, by this light of heaven,   150
I know not how I lost him. Here I kneel:
If e'er my will did trespass 'gainst his love,
Either in discourse of thought or actual deed,

Or that mine eyes, mine ears, or any sense,
Delighted them in any other form;
Or that I do not yet, and ever did,
And ever will — though he do shake me off
To beggarly divorcement — love him dearly,
Comfort forswear me!   Unkindness may do much;
And his unkindness may defeat my life,   160
But never taint my love.   I cannot say "whore":
It doth abhor me now I speak the word;
To do the act that might the addition earn
Not the world's mass of vanity could make me.
   Iago.   I pray you, be content; 't is but his
         humour:
The business of the state does him offence,
And he does chide with you.
   Des.   If 't were not other, —
   Iago.   'T is but so, I warrant.
                              [*Trumpets within.*
Hark, how those instruments summon to supper!
The messengers of Venice stay the meat: 170
Go in, and weep not; all things shall be well.
                    [*Exeunt Desdemona and Emilia.*

                    Enter Roderigo

How now, Roderigo!
   Rod.   I do not find that thou dealest justly with
         me.
   Iago.   What in the contrary?
   Rod.   Every day thou daffest me with some device, Iago; and rather, as it seems to me now, keep-
est from me all conveniency than suppliest me with
the least advantage of hope.   I will indeed no longer

endure it, nor am I yet persuaded to put up in peace
what already I have foolishly suffered.   182

Iago.   Will you hear me, Roderigo?

Rod.   'Faith, I have heard too much, for your
words and performances are no kin together.

Iago.   You charge me most unjustly.

Rod.   With nought but truth.   I have wasted myself out of my means.   The jewels you have had from
me to deliver to Desdemona would half have corrupted a votarist: you have told me she hath received
them and returned me expectations and comforts of
sudden respect and acquaintance, but I find none.   193

Iago.   Well; go to; very well.

Rod.   Very well! go to! I cannot go to, man; nor
't is not very well: nay, I think it is scurvy, and
begin to find myself fopped in it.

Iago.   Very well.

Rod.   I tell you 't is not very well.   I will make
myself known to Desdemona: if she will return me
my jewels, I will give over my suit and repent my
unlawful solicitation; if not, assure yourself I will
seek satisfaction of you.   203

Iago.   You have said now.

Rod.   Ay, and said nothing but what I protest
intendment of doing.

Iago.   Why, now I see there 's mettle in thee, and
even from this instant do build on thee a better
opinion than ever before.   Give me thy hand, Roderigo: thou hast taken against me a most just exception; but yet, I protest, I have dealt most directly
in thy affair.

Rod.   It hath not appeared.

Iago. I grant indeed it hath not appeared, and 213
your suspicion is not without wit and judgement.
But, Roderigo, if thou hast that in thee indeed,
which I have greater reason to believe now than
ever, I mean purpose, courage and valour, this night
show it: if thou the next night following enjoy not
Desdemona, take me from this world with treachery
and devise engines for my life.   222

Rod. Well, what is it? is it within reason and compass?

Iago. Sir, there is especial commission come from
Venice to depute Cassio in Othello's place.

Rod. Is that true? why, then Othello and Desdemona return again to Venice.

Iago. O, no; he goes into Mauritania and takes
away with him the fair Desdemona, unless his abode
be lingered here by some accident: wherein none can
be so determinate as the removing of Cassio.   233

Rod. How do you mean, removing of him?

Iago. Why, by making him uncapable of Othello's
place; knocking out his brains.

Rod. And that you would have me do?

Iago. Ay, if you dare do yourself a profit and a
right. He sups to-night with a harlotry, and thither
will I go to him: he knows not yet of his honourable
fortune. If you will watch his going thence, which
I will fashion to fall out between twelve and one,
you may take him at your pleasure: I will be near
to second your attempt, and he shall fall between us.
Come, stand not amazed at it, but go along with me;
I will show you such a necessity in his death that
you shall think yourself bound to put it on him.

It is now high supper-time, and the night grows to
waste: about it.   250

    Rod.   I will hear further reason for this.

    Iago.   And you shall be satisfied. `   [*Exeunt.*

SCENE III — *Another room in the castle*

Enter OTHELLO, LODOVICO, DESDEMONA, EMILIA,
        and Attendants

    Lod.   I do beseech you, sir, trouble yourself no
        further.

    Oth.   O, pardon me; 't will do me good to walk.

    Lod.   Madam, good night; I humbly thank your
        ladyship.

    Des.   Your honour is most welcome.

    Oth.   Will you walk, sir?
O, — Desdemona, —

    Des.   My lord?

    Oth.   Get you to bed on the instant; I will be
returned forthwith: dismiss your attendant there:
look it be done.

    Des.   I will, my lord.   `   10
          [*Exeunt Othello, Lodovico, and Attendants.*

    Emil.   How goes it now? he looks gentler than he
        did.

    Des.   He says he will return incontinent:
He hath commanded me to go to bed,
And bade me to dismiss you.

    Emil.   Dismiss me!

    Des.   It was his bidding; therefore, good Emilia,
Give me my nightly wearing, and adieu:
We must not now displease him.

    Emil.   I would you had never seen him!

    Des.   So would not I: my love doth so approve
        him,

That even his stubbornness, his checks, his frowns, —

Prithee, unpin me, — have grace and favour in them. 21

    Emil.   I have laid those sheets you bade me on the
        bed.

    Des.   All 's one. Good faith, how foolish are our
        minds!

If I do die before thee, prithee, shroud me

In one of those same sheets.

    Emil.   Come, come, you talk.

    Des.   My mother had a maid call'd Barbara:

She was in love, and he she loved proved mad

And did forsake her: she had a song of "willow";

An old thing 't was, but it express'd her fortune,

And she died singing it: that song to-night   30

Will not go from my mind; I have much to do

But to go hang my head all at one side,

And sing it like poor Barbara. Prithee, dispatch.

    Emil.   Shall I go fetch your night-gown?

    Des.   No, unpin me here.

This Lodovico is a proper man.

    Emil.   A very handsome man.

    Des.   He speaks well.

    Emil.   I know a lady in Venice would have walked

barefoot to Palestine for a touch of his nether lip. 40

    Des.   [*Singing*] The poor soul sat sighing by a
        sycamore tree,

    Sing all a green willow;

Her hand on her bosom, her head on her knee,

    Sing willow, willow, willow:

The fresh streams ran by her, and murmur'd her
      moans;
  Sing willow, willow, willow;
  Her salt tears fell from her, and soften'd the
      stones; —
Lay by these: —
[*Singing*] Sing willow, willow, willow;
Prithee, hie thee; he 'll come anon: —   50
[*Singing*] Sing all a green willow must be my garland.
  Let nobody blame him; his scorn I approve, —
Nay, that 's not next — Hark! who is 't that knocks?
    Emil.   It 's the wind.
    Des. [*Singing*] I call'd my love false love; but
      what said he then?
  Sing willow, willow, willow:
  If I court moe women, you 'll couch with moe
      men. —
So, get thee gone; good night. Mine eyes do itch;
Doth that bode weeping?
    Emil.   'T is neither here nor there.
    Des.   I have heard it said so. O, these men, these
      men!   60
Dost thou in conscience think, — tell me, Emilia, —
That there be women do abuse their husbands
In such gross kind?
    Emil.   There be some such, no question.
    Des.   Wouldst thou do such a deed for all the
      world?
    Emil.   Why, would not you?
    Des.   No, by this heavenly light!
    Emil.   Nor I neither by this heavenly light;
I might do 't as well i' the dark.

Des. Wouldst thou do such a deed for all the
  world?

Emil. The world 's a huge thing: it is a great
  price.

For a small vice.

Des.   In truth, I think thou wouldst not.   70

Emil. In troth, I think I should; and undo 't
when I had done. Marry, I would not do such a
thing for a joint-ring, nor for measures of lawn, nor
for gowns, petticoats, nor caps, nor any petty exhibition; but, for the whole world, — why, who would
not make her husband a cuckold to make him a
monarch? I should venture purgatory for 't.

Des. Beshrew me, if I would do such a wrong
For the whole world.   79

Emil. Why, the wrong is but a wrong i' the world;
and having the world for your labour, 't is a wrong
in your own world, and you might quickly make it
right.

Des. I do not think there is any such woman.

Emil. Yes, a dozen; and as many to the vantage as
would store the world they played for.
But I do think it is their husbands' faults
If wives do fall: say that they slack their duties,
And pour our treasures into foreign laps,
Or else break out in peevish jealousies,   90
Throwing restraint upon us; or say they strike us,
Or scant our former having in despite;
Why, we have galls, and though we have some grace,
Yet have we some revenge.   Let husbands know
Their wives have sense like them: they see and smell
And have their palates both for sweet and sour,

As husbands have.   What is it that they do
When they change us for others?   Is it sport?
I think it is: and doth affection breed it?
I think it doth: is 't frailty that thus errs?   100
It is so too: and have not we affections,
Desires for sport, and frailty, as men have?
Then let them use us well: else let them know,
The ills we do, their ills instruct us so.

  Des.   Good night, good night: heaven me such
    uses send,
  Not to pick bad from bad, but by bad mend!
            [*Exeunt.*

ACT V

SCENE I — *Cyprus.   A street*

Enter IAGO and RODERIGO

  Iago.   Here, stand behind this bulk; straight will
    he come:
Wear thy good rapier bare, and put it home:
Quick, quick; fear nothing; I 'll be at thy elbow:
It makes us, or it mars us; think on that,
And fix most firm thy resolution.

  Rod.   Be near at hand; I may miscarry in 't.

  Iago.   Here, at thy hand: be bold, and take thy
    stand.   [*Retires.*

  Rod.   I have no great devotion to the deed;
And yet he hath given me satisfying reasons:
'T is but a man gone.   Forth, my sword: he dies.   10

  Iago.   I have rubb'd this young quat almost to
    the sense,

And he grows angry.   Now, whether he kill Cassio,
Or Cassio him, or each do kill the other,
Every way makes my gain: live Roderigo,
He calls me to a restitution large
Of gold and jewels that I bobb'd from him,
As gifts to Desdemona;
It must not be: if Cassio do remain,
He hath a daily beauty in his life
That makes me ugly; and, besides, the Moor   20
May unfold me to him; there stand I in much peril:
No, he must die.   But so: I hear him coming.

Enter Cassio

Rod.   I know his gait, 't is he. — Villain, thou
        diest!
                        [*Makes a pass at Cassio.*
Cas.   That thrust had been mine enemy indeed,
But that my coat is better than thou know'st:
I will make proof of thine.
                        [*Draws, and wounds Roderigo.*
Rod.   O, I am slain!
                        [*Iago from behind wounds Cassio in the
                                        leg, and exit.*
Cas.   I am maim'd for ever.   Help, ho! murder!
        murder!   [*Falls.*

Enter Othello

Oth.   The voice of Cassio: Iago keeps his word.
Rod.   O, villain that I am!
Oth.   It is even so.
Cas.   O, help, ho! light! a surgeon!   30
Oth.   'T is he: — O brave Iago, honest and just,

That hast such noble sense of thy friend's wrong!
Thou teachest me.   Minion, your dear lies dead,
And your unblest fate hies: strumpet, I come.
Forth of my heart those charms, thine eyes, are
          blotted;
Thy bed, lust-stain'd, shall with lust's blood be
          spotted.   [*Exit.*

Enter LODOVICO *and* GRATIANO

Cas.   What ho! no watch? no passage? murder!
          murder!
Gra.   'T is some mischance; the cry is very direful.
Cas.   O, help!
Lod.   Hark!   40
Rod.   O wretched villain!
Lod.   Two or three groan: it is a heavy night:
These may be counterfeits: let 's think 't unsafe
To come in to the cry without more help.
Rod.   Nobody come? then shall I bleed to death.
Lod.   Hark!

Re-enter IAGO, *with a light*

Gra.   Here 's one comes in his shirt, with light
          and weapons.
Iago.   Who 's there? whose noise is this that cries
          on murder?
Lod.   We do not know.
Iago.   Did not you hear a cry?
Cas.   Here, here! for heaven's sake, help me!
Iago.   What 's the matter?   50
Gra.   This is Othello's ancient, as I take it.
Lod.   The same indeed; a very valiant fellow.
Iago.   What are you here that cry so grievously?

   Cas.   Iago?   O, I am spoil'd, undone by villains!
Give me some help.

   Iago.   O me, lieutenant! what villains have done
     this?

   Cas.   I think that one of them is hereabout,
And cannot make away.

   Iago.   O treacherous villains!
What are you there? come in, and give some help.
                          [*To Lodovico and Gratiano.*

   Rod.   O, help me here!   60
   Cas.   That's one of them.
   Iago.   O murderous slave!   O villain!
                       [*Stabs Roderigo.*

   Rod.   O damn'd Iago!   O inhuman dog!
   Iago.   Kill men i' the dark! — Where be these
     bloody thieves? —
How silent is this town! — Ho! murder! murder! —
What may you be? are you of good or evil?

   Lod.   As you shall prove us, praise us.
   Iago.   Signior Lodovico?
   Lod.   He, sir.
   Iago.   I cry you mercy.   Here's Cassio hurt by
     villains.

   Gra.   Cassio!   70
   Iago.   How is 't, brother!
   Cas.   My leg is cut in two.
   Iago.   Marry, heaven forbid!
Light, gentlemen: I'll bind it with my shirt.

Enter BIANCA

   Bian.   What is the matter, ho? who is 't that
     cried?

Iago.   Who is 't that cried!

Bian.   O my dear Cassio! my sweet Cassio!
O Cassio, Cassio, Cassio!

Iago.   O notable strumpet! Cassio, may you sus-
        pect

Who they should be that have thus mangled you?

Cas.   No.   80

Gra.   I am sorry to find you thus: I have been to
        seek you.

Iago.   Lend me a garter. So. O, for a chair,
To bear him easily hence!

Bian.   Alas, he faints! O Cassio, Cassio, Cassio!

Iago.   Gentlemen all, I do suspect this trash
To be a party in this injury.
Patience awhile, good Cassio. Come, come;
Lend me a light. Know we this face or no?
Alas, my friend and my dear countryman
Roderigo! no: — yes, sure: — O heaven! Roderigo.   90

Gra.   What, of Venice?

Iago.   Even he, sir: did you know him?

Gra.   Know him! ay.

Iago.   Signior Gratiano? I cry you gentle pardon;
These bloody accidents must excuse my manners,
That so neglected you.

Gra.   I am glad to see you.

Iago.   How do you, Cassio? O, a chair, a chair!

Gra.   Roderigo!

Iago.   He, he, 't is he. [*A chair brought in.*] O,
        that 's well said; the chair.

Some good man bear him carefully from hence;
I 'll fetch the general's surgeon. [*To Bianca*] For
        you, mistress,   100

Save you your labour.   He that lies slain here, Cassio,
Was my dear friend: what malice was between you?
   Cas.   None in the world; nor do I know the man.
   Iago.   [*To Bian.*]   What, look you pale?   O, bear
      him out o' the air.
               [*Cassio and Roderigo are borne off.*
Stay you, good gentlemen.   Look you pale, mistress?
Do you perceive the gastness of her eye?
Nay, if you stare, we shall hear more anon.
Behold her well; I pray you, look upon her:
Do you see, gentlemen? nay, guiltiness will speak,
Though tongues were out of use.   110

Enter EMILIA

   Emil.   'Las, what 's the matter?   what 's the
      matter, husband?
   Iago.   Cassio hath here been set on in the dark
By Roderigo and fellows that are scaped:
He 's almost slain, and Roderigo dead.
   Emil.   Alas, good gentleman! alas, good Cassio!
   Iago.   This is the fruit of whoring.   Prithee,
      Emilia,
Go know of Cassio where he supp'd to-night.
[*To Bianca*] What, do you shake at that?
   Bian.   He supp'd at my house; but I therefore
      shake not.
   Iago.   O, did he so?   I charge you, go with 120
      me.
   Emil.   Fie, fie upon thee, strumpet!
   Bian.   I am no strumpet; but of life as honest
As you that thus abuse me.
   Emil.   As I! foh! fie upon thee!

Iago. Kind gentlemen, let 's go see poor Cassio
      dress'd.
Come, mistress, you must tell 's another tale.
Emilia, run you to the citadel,
And tell my lord and lady what hath happ'd.
Will you go on? I pray. [*Aside*] This is the night
That either makes me or fordoes me quite. [*Exeunt.*

SCENE II — *A bedchamber in the castle:* DESDEMONA
in bed asleep; a light burning

Enter OTHELLO

Oth. It is the cause, it is the cause, my soul, —
Let me not name it to you, you chaste stars! —
It is the cause. Yet I 'll not shed her blood,
Nor scar that whiter skin of hers than snow,
And smooth as monumental alabaster.
Yet she must die, else she 'll betray more men.
Put out the light, and then put out the light:
If I quench thee, thou flaming minister,
I can again thy former light restore.
Should I repent me: but once put out thy light,   10
Thou cunning'st pattern of excelling nature,
I know not where is that Promethean heat
That can thy light relume. When I have pluck'd
      the rose,
I cannot give it vital growth again,
It must needs wither: I 'll smell it on the tree.
                    [*Kissing her.*
Ah, balmy breath, that dost almost persuade
Justice to break her sword! One more, one more,
Be thus when thou art dead, and I will kill thee,

And love thee after.   One more, and this the last:
So sweet was ne'er so fatal.   I must weep,   20
But they are cruel tears: this sorrow's heavenly;
It strikes where it doth love.   She wakes.

   Des.   Who 's there?   Othello?
   Oth.   Ay, Desdemona.
   Des.   Will you come to bed, my lord?
   Oth.   Have you pray'd to-night, Desdemona?
   Des.   Ay, my lord.
   Oth.   If you bethink yourself of any crime
Unreconciled as yet to heaven and grace,
Solicit for it straight.
   Des.   Alas, my lord, what do you mean by that?
   Oth.   Well, do it, and be brief; I will walk by: 30
I would not kill thy unprepared spirit;
No; heaven forfend! I would not kill thy soul.
   Des.   Talk you of killing?
   Oth.   Ay, I do.
   Des.   Then heaven
Have mercy on me!
   Oth.   Amen, with all my heart!
   Des.   If you say so, I hope you will not kill me.
   Oth.   Hum!
   Des.   And yet I fear you; for you are fatal then
When your eyes roll so: why I should fear I know
       not,
Since guiltiness I know not; but yet I feel I fear.
   Oth.   Think on thy sins.
   Des.   They are loves I bear to you.
   Oth.   Ay, and for that thou diest.   41
   Des.   That death 's unnatural that kills for loving.
Alas, why gnaw you so your nether lip?

Some bloody passion shakes your very frame:
These are portents; but yet I hope, I hope,
They do not point on me.

   Oth.   Peace, and be still!

   Des. I will so. What 's the matter?

   Oth. That handkerchief which I so love and gave
       thee
Thou gavest to Cassio.

   Des.   No, by my life and soul!
Send for the man, and ask him.

   Oth.   Sweet soul, take heed,
Take heed of perjury; thou art on thy death-bed.   51

   Des. Ay, but not yet to die.

   Oth.   Yes, presently:
Therefore confess thee freely of thy sin;
For to deny each article with oath
Cannot remove nor choke the strong conception
That I do groan withal. Thou art to die.

   Des. Then Lord have mercy on me!

   Oth.   I say, amen.

   Des. And have you mercy too! I never did
Offend you in my life; never loved Cassio
But with such general warranty of heaven   60
As I might love; I never gave him token.

   Oth. By heaven, I saw my handkerchief in 's hand.
O perjured woman! thou dost stone my heart,
And makest me call what I intend to do
A murder, which I thought a sacrifice:
I saw the handkerchief.

   Des.   He found it then;
I never gave it him: send for him hither;
Let him confess a truth.

Oth.   He hath confess'd.

Des. What, my lord?

Oth. That he hath used thee.

Des.   How? unlawfully?

Oth.   Ay. 70

Des. He will not say so.

Oth.   No, his mouth is stopp'd;
Honest Iago hath ta'en order for 't.

Des. O! my fear interprets: what, is he dead?

Oth. Had all his hairs been lives, my great
     revenge
Had stomach for them all.

Des. Alas! he is betray'd and I undone.

Oth. Out, strumpet! weep'st thou for him to my
     face?

Des. O, banish me, my lord, but kill me not!

Oth. Down, strumpet!

Des. Kill me to-morrow: let me live to-night!   80

Oth. Nay, if you strive, —

Des. But half an hour!

Oth.   Being done, there is no pause.

Des. But while I say one prayer!

Oth.   It is too late.

                              [*He stifles her.*

Emil. [*Within*] My lord, my lord! what, ho! my
     lord, my lord!

Oth. What noise is this? Not dead? not yet
     quite dead?
I that am cruel am yet merciful;
I would not have thee linger in thy pain:
So, so.

Emil. [*Within*] What, ho! my lord, my lord!

Oth.   Who 's there?

Emil.   [*Within*]   O, good my lord, I would speak
          a word with you!   90

Oth.   Yes: 't is Emilia.   By and by.   She 's dead.
'T is like she comes to speak of Cassio's death. —
The noise was here.   Ha! no more moving?
Still as the grave.   Shall she come in? were 't good? —
I think she stirs again: — no.   What 's best to do?
If she come in, she 'll sure speak to my wife:
My wife! my wife! what wife? I have no wife.
O, insupportable!   O heavy hour!
Methinks it should be now a huge eclipse
Of sun and moon, and that the affrighted globe   100
Should yawn at alteration.

Emil.   [*Within*] I do beseech you
That I may speak with you, O, good my lord!

Oth.   I had forgot thee: O, come in, Emilia:
Soft; by and by.   Let me the curtains draw.
Where art thou?   [*Unlocks the door.*

                    Enter EMILIA

                What 's the matter with thee now?

Emil.   O, my good lord, yonder 's foul murders
          done!

Oth.   What, now?

Emil.   But now, my lord.

Oth.   It is the very error of the moon;
She comes more nearer earth than she was wont,   110
And makes men mad.

Emil.   Cassio, my lord, hath kill'd a young Vene-
          tian
Call'd Roderigo.

Oth.   Roderigo kill'd!
And Cassio kill'd!

Emil.   No, Cassio is not kill'd.

Oth.   Not Cassio kill'd! then murder 's out of tune,
And sweet revenge grows harsh.

Des.   O, falsely, falsely murder'd!

Emil.   Alas, what cry is that?

Oth.   That! what?

Emil.   Out, and alas! that was my lady's voice.
Help! help, ho! help!   O lady, speak again!   120
Sweet Desdemona! O sweet mistress, speak!

Des.   A guiltless death I die.

Emil.   O, who hath done this deed?

Des.   Nobody; I myself.   Farewell:
Commend me to my kind lord: O farewell!   [*Dies.*

Oth.   Why, how should she be murder'd?

Emil.   Alas, who knows?

Oth.   You heard her say herself, it was not I.

Emil.   She said so: I must needs report the truth.

Oth.   She 's like a liar gone to burning hell:
'T was I that kill'd her.

Emil.   O, the more angel she,   130
And you the blacker devil!

Oth.   She turn'd to folly, and she was a whore.

Emil.   Thou dost belie her, and thou art a devil.

Oth.   She was false as water.

Emil.   Thou art rash as fire, to say
That she was false: O, she was heavenly true!

Oth.   Cassio did top her; ask thy husband else.
O, I were damn'd beneath all depth in hell,
But that I did proceed upon just grounds
To this extremity.   Thy husband knew it all.

Emil.   My husband!   140

Oth.   Thy husband.

Emil.   That she was false to wedlock?

Oth.   Ay, with Cassio.   Nay, had she been true,
If heaven would make me such another world
Of one entire and perfect chrysolite,
I 'ld not have sold her for it.

Emil.   My husband!

Oth.   Ay, 't was he that told me first:
An honest man he is, and hates the slime
That sticks on filthy deeds.

Emil.   My husband!

Oth.   What needs this iteration, woman?   I say
          thy husband.   150

Emil.   O mistress, villany hath made mocks with
          love!
My husband say that she was false!

Oth.   He, woman;
I say thy husband: dost understand the word?
My friend, thy husband, honest honest Iago.

Emil.   If he say so, may his pernicious soul
Rot half a grain a day! he lies to the heart:
She was too fond of her most filthy bargain.

Oth.   Ha!

Emil.   Do thy worst:
This deed of thine is no more worthy heaven   160
Than thou wast worthy her.

Oth.   Peace, you were best.

Emil.   Thou hast not half that power to do me
          harm
As I have to be hurt.   O gull! O dolt!
As ignorant as dirt! thou hast done a deed —

I care not for thy sword; I 'll make thee known,
Though I lost twenty lives.—Help! help, ho! help!
The Moor hath kill'd my mistress! Murder! murder!

Enter Montano, Gratiano, Iago, *and others*

Mon. What is the matter? How now, general!
Emil. O, are you come, Iago? you have done well,
That men must lay their murders on your neck.   170
Gra. What is the matter?
Emil. Disprove this villain, if thou be'st a man:
He says thou told'st him that his wife was false:
I know thou didst not, thou 'rt not such a villain:
Speak, for my heart is full.
Iago. I told him what I thought, and told no
          more
Than what he found himself was apt and true.
Emil. But did you ever tell him she was false?
Iago. I did.
Emil. You told a lie; an odious, damned lie;   180
Upon my soul, a lie, a wicked lie.
She false with Cassio! — did you say with Cassio?
Iago. With Cassio, mistress. Go to, charm your
          tongue.
Emil. I will not charm my tongue; I am bound
          to speak:
My mistress here lies murder'd in her bed, —
All. O heavens forfend!
Emil. And your reports have set the murder on.
Oth. Nay, stare not, masters: it is true, indeed.
Gra. 'T is a strange truth.
Mon. O monstrous act!
Emil.   Villany, villany, villany!   190

I think upon 't: I think: I smell 't: O villany! —
I thought so then: — I 'll kill myself for grief: —
O villany, villany!

    Iago.   What, are you mad? I charge you, get you
        home.

    Emil.   Good gentlemen, let me have leave to
        speak:

'T is proper I obey him, but not now.
Perchance, Iago, I will ne'er go home.

    Oth.   O! O! O!   *[He falls on the bed.*

    Emil.   Nay, lay thee down and roar;
For thou hast kill'd the sweetest innocent
That e'er did lift up eye.

    Oth.   *[Rising]* O, she was foul!   200
I scarce did know you, uncle: there lies your niece,
Whose breath, indeed, these hands have newly
        stopp'd:
I know this act shows horrible and grim.

    Gra.   Poor Desdemona! I am glad thy father 's
        dead:

Thy match was mortal to him, and pure grief
Shore his old thread in twain: did he live now,
This sight would make him do a desperate turn,
Yea, curse his better angel from his side,
And fall to reprobation.

    Oth.   'T is pitiful; but yet Iago knows   210
That she with Cassio hath the act of shame
A thousand times committed; Cassio confess'd it:
And she did gratify his amorous works
With that recognizance and pledge of love
Which I first gave her; I saw it in his hand:
It was a handkerchief, an antique token

My father gave my mother.

 Emil. O heaven! O heavenly powers!

 Iago. Come, hold your peace.

 Emil.   'T will out, 't will out: I peace!

No, I will speak as liberal as the north: 220

Let heaven and men and devils, let them all,

All, all, cry shame against me, yet I 'll speak.

 Iago. Be wise, and get you home.

 Emil.   I will not.

      [Iago offers to stab Emilia.

 Gra.   Fie!

Your sword upon a woman?

 Emil. O thou dull Moor! that handkerchief thou

   speak'st of

I found by fortune and did give my husband;

For often with a solemn earnestness,

More than indeed belong'd to such a trifle,

He begg'd o' me to steal it.

 Iago.   Villanous whore!

 Emil. She give it Cassio! no, alas! I found it, 230

And I did give 't my husband.

 Iago.   Filth, thou liest!

 Emil. By heaven, I do not, I do not, gentlemen.

O murderous coxcomb! what should such a fool

Do with so good a wife?

 Oth.   Are there no stones in heaven

But what serve for the thunder? — Precious villain!

  [He runs at Iago; Iago, from behind, stabs Emilia,

            and exit.

 Gra. The woman falls; sure, he hath kill'd his

   wife.

 Emil. Ay, ay: O, lay me by my mistress' side.

Gra. He 's gone, but his wife 's kill'd.

Mon. 'T is a notorious villain.   Take you this
    weapon,

Which I have here recover'd from the Moor: 240

Come, guard the door without; let him not pass,

But kill him rather.   I 'll after that same villain,

For 't is a damned slave.

                    [*Exeunt Montano and Gratiano.*

Oth.   I am not valiant neither,

But every puny whipster gets my sword:

But why should honour outlive honesty?

Let it go all.

Emil.   What did thy song bode, lady?

Hark, canst thou hear me?   I will play the swan,

And die in music.   [*Singing*] Willow, willow,
    willow. —

Moor, she was chaste; she loved thee, cruel Moor;

So come my soul to bliss, as I speak true;   250

So speaking as I think, I die, I die.   [*Dies.*

Oth.   I have another weapon in this chamber;

It is a sword of Spain, the ice-brook's temper: —

O, here it is.   Uncle, I must come forth.

Gra.   [*Within*] If thou attempt it, it will cost thee
    dear:

Thou hast no weapon, and perforce must suffer.

Oth.   Look in upon me then and speak with
    me,

Or, naked as I am, I will assault thee.

            Re-enter GRATIANO

Gra.   What is the matter?

Oth.   Behold, I have a weapon;

A better never did itself sustain   260
Upon a soldier's thigh: I have seen the day,
That, with this little arm and this good sword,
I have made my way through more impediments
Than twenty times your stop: but, O vain boast!
Who can control his fate? 't is not so now.
Be not afraid, though you do see me weapon'd;
Here is my journey's end, here is my butt,
And very sea-mark of my utmost sail.
Do you go back dismay'd? 't is a lost fear;
Man but a rush against Othello's breast,   270
And he retires.   Where should Othello go?
Now, how dost thou look now?   O ill-starr'd wench!
Pale as thy smock! when we shall meet at compt,
This look of thine will hurl my soul from heaven,
And fiends will snatch at it.   Cold, cold, my girl!
Even like thy chastity.   O cursed slave!
Whip me, ye devils,
From the possession of this heavenly sight!
Blow me about in winds! roast me in sulphur!
Wash me in steep-down gulfs of liquid fire!   280
O Desdemona! Desdemona! dead!
Oh! Oh! Oh!

Enter Lodovico, Montano, Cassio *carried in a chair,
        and* Officers *with* Iago, *prisoner*

    Lod. Where is this rash and most unfortunate
        man?
    Oth. That 's he that was Othello: here I am.
    Lod. Where is that viper? bring the villain forth.
    Oth. I look down towards his feet; but that 's
        a fable.

If that thou be'st a devil, I cannot kill thee.

[Wounds Iago.

   Lod.   Wrench his sword from him.

   Iago.   I bleed, sir; but not kill'd.

   Oth.   I am not sorry neither: I 'ld have thee
       live;

For, in my sense, 't is happiness to die.   290

   Lod.   O thou Othello, that wert once so good,

Fall'n in the practice of a damned slave,

What shall be said to thee?

   Oth.   Why, any thing:

An honourable murderer, if you will;

For nought I did in hate, but all in honour.

   Lod.   This wretch hath part confess'd his villany:

Did you and he consent in Cassio's death?

   Oth.   Ay.

   Cas.   Dear general, I never gave you cause.

   Oth.   I do believe it, and I ask you pardon.   300

Will you, I pray, demand that demi-devil

Why he hath thus ensnared my soul and body?

   Iago.   Demand me nothing: what you know, you
       know:

From this time forth I never will speak word.

   Lod.   What, not to pray?

   Gra.   Torments will ope your lips.

   Oth.   Well, thou dost best.

   Lod.   Sir, you shall understand what hath befall'n,

Which, as I think, you know not. Here is a letter

Found in the pocket of the slain Roderigo;

And here another: the one of them imports   310

The death of Cassio to be undertook

By Roderigo.

Oth.   O villain!

Cas.   Most heathenish and most gross!

Lod.   Now here 's another discontented paper,
Found in his pocket too; and this, it seems,
Roderigo meant to have sent this damned villain;
But that belike Iago in the interim
Came in and satisfied him.

Oth.   O the pernicious caitiff!
How came you, Cassio, by that handkerchief
That was my wife's?

Cas.   I found it in my chamber: 320
And he himself confess'd but even now
That there he dropp'd it for a special purpose
Which wrought to his desire.

Oth.   . O fool! fool! fool!

Cas.   There is besides in Roderigo's letter,
How he upbraids Iago, that he made him
Brave me upon the watch; whereon it came
That I was cast: and even but now he spake,
After long seeming dead, Iago hurt him,
Iago set him on.

Lod.   You must forsake this room, and go with
          us:
Your power and your command is taken off,   331
And Cassio rules in Cyprus.   For this slave,
If there be any cunning cruelty
That can torment him much and hold him long,
It shall be his.   You shall close prisoner rest,
Till that the nature of your fault be known
To the Venetian state.   Come, bring him away.

Oth.   Soft you; a word or two before you go.
I have done the state some service, and they know 't.

No more of that.   I pray you, in your letters,   340
When you shall these unlucky deeds relate,
Speak of me as I am; nothing extenuate,
Nor set down aught in malice: then must you speak
Of one that loved not wisely but too well;
Of one not easily jealous, but, being wrought,
Perplex'd in the extreme; of one whose hand,
Like the base Indian, threw a pearl away
Richer than all his tribe; of one whose subdued
          eyes,
Albeit unused to the melting mood,
Drop tears as fast as the Arabian trees   350
Their medicinal gum.   Set you down this;
And say besides, that in Aleppo once,
Where a malignant and a turban'd Turk
Beat a Venetian and traduced the state,
I took by the throat the circumcised dog,
And smote him, thus.   [*Stabs himself.*

   Lod.   O bloody period!
   Gra.   All that 's spoke is marr'd.
   Oth.   I kiss'd thee ere I kill'd thee: no way but
          this;
Killing myself, to die upon a kiss.

          [*Falls on the bed, and dies.*

   Cas.   This did I fear, but thought he had no
          weapon;
For he was great of heart.
   Lod.   [*To Iago*]   O Spartan dog,   361
More fell than anguish, hunger, or the sea!
Look on the tragic loading of this bed;
This is thy work: the object poisons sight;
Let it be hid.   Gratiano, keep the house,

And seize upon the fortunes of the Moor,
For they succeed on you.   To you, lord governor,
Remains the censure of this hellish villain;
The time, the place, the torture: O, enforce it!
Myself will straight aboard; and to the state   370
This heavy act with heavy heart relate.   [*Exeunt.*

NOTES

[References to Abbott are to his
Shakespearian Grammar, 1869, etc.]

ACT I — SCENE 1

The first scene introduces us at once to the man who is, single-handed, to contrive the tragic harms, and allows us a brief, vivid glimpse of his two principal victims, whose midnight match has just opened the action. Iago's malicious portrait of Cassio gives us a preliminary notion of his principal tool; while his treatment of the poor dupe Roderigo prepares us for his more diabolical machination in the main plot.

3. *this,* the intended elopement. Roderigo, having paid Iago to further his suit to Desdemona, assumes that he has been playing a double game. It does not suit Iago at this stage to throw off the mask.

8 f. By way of proving that he has not been secretly in league, as Roderigo suspects, with the successful suitor, Iago relates a signal humiliation he has suffered at Othello's hands by his appointment of Cassio as lieutenant. The incident related illustrates Othello's high prestige at Venice, and prepares us for his easy victory in the Senate in i. 3.

bombast circumstance, pompous circumlocution.

19. Iago professes to deride Cassio as a mere arm-chair strategist, who understood nothing of war but its theoretic calculations. Mercutio similarly scoffs at "one that fights by the book of arithmetic" (*Romeo and Juliet*). As to the value of his character of Cassio, see Introduction, § 8.

20. *a Florentine.* Florence was reputed one of the capitals of Italian commerce (cf. the coin *florin*); Iago avails himself of this association to clinch his character of Cassio as a mere man of figures — a "book-keeper" in respect of soldiership, as "a Florentine" was likely to be.

21. *A fellow almost damned in a fair wife.* No interpretation of this line is quite satisfactory, and no emendation that is even plausible has been proposed. As it stands, the text has an air of hinting at Cassio's marked susceptibility to the attraction of women, a trait of which Iago is later to make effective use. But the charge against him both in v. 19 before, and in vv. 22–26 after this line, is the quite distinct, though compatible, one of being a bookish theorist; and it is difficult to believe that v. 24 interrupted, instead of supported, this thought.

25. *toged consuls,* here of the counsellors of the Venetian senate in their gowns, a purely civilian body. For "consuls" so applied, cf. i. 2. 43: "many of the consuls," &c.

39. *Whether . . . affined,* whether I stand in so close a relation to him as to be bound (to love him).

44. *you shall mark;* the use of "shall" in phrases of this type is colored by its original sense of "be bound, owe." "You are sure to." Cf. Abbott, § 315.

49. *me,* the colloquial "ethical dative." Abbott, § 220.

50. *visages,* outer semblances.

57. *Were I,* &c., if I were chief, I would promptly throw off the "shows of service" which I now practice for my own ends, and which are taken to reflect my character.

61 f. *when my outward action, i. e.* you may as soon expect to find me a weak sentimentalist, the sport of every fool, as a man who sincerely means the deference he professes.

66. *owe,* possess.

66. *thick-lips.* One of several indications that Shakespeare drew no distinction between the Moorish and the negro types. See Introduction, p. xvii, note.

68. *Rouse him,* &c. The first "him" refers naturally to Brabantio, the second and following pronouns to Othello. Iago betrays his real animus by this instant reversion to the object of it. The rousing of the father interests him only as the means of "poisoning" Othello's "delight."

99. *distempering,* intoxicating.

100. *Upon malicious bravery,* in . . . defiance.

106. *a grange,* a farm-house.

107. *In simple . . . soul,* in perfect sincerity of purpose.

112. *nephews,* grandsons. The word was currently used both thus and for "cousin," as well as for a brother's or sister's child. Shakespeare in his will refers to his grand-daughter, Elizabeth Hall, as his *niece.*

124. *At this odd-even . . . night,* the time about midnight, a singular and nondescript interval, half-way between the beginning and the end of the night.

126. *gondolier,* probably to be scanned góndeler, like píoner, énginer, &c.

128. *your allowance,* what you approve.

132. *from,* contrary to, in violation of.

136. *Tying ... in,* tying them up in, giving him complete possession of them.

137. *extravagant and wheeling,* wandering and gad-about.

146. Iago disdains to use his customary dissimulation with a Roderigo; his motive for getting away before Brabantio appears is the true one. He wants to damage Othello, but he knows that for the moment the stroke will only "gall" him, since the government imperatively need his services, and that he himself cannot therefore break with him.

159. *the Sagittary.* Shakespeare doubtless meant this (here and in i. 3. 115) to be the name of an inn; it is immaterial that no such name is recorded among the Venetian inns of that date.

161 f. Brabantio's almost incoherent anger helps to drive home two points important for the sequel: (1) that Desdemona's marriage was, to Venetian ideas, a very strange and even revolting one; (2) that she had deceived her father. The second of these prepares us for his parting shaft as he leaves the Senate, "She has deceived her father, and may thee." Brabantio's rage is not mere bluster. The blow of Desdemona's marriage "was mortal to him, and pure grief shore his old thread in twain"; he died at most a few days later, as Gratiano (the "brother" of v. 177) relates at the close (v. 2. 205).

172. *Is there not charms.* On this *is* with a plural, cf. Abbott, § 335. It occurs mainly where the subject follows, and where its plurality is unimportant. It is thus better explained as a construction according to the sense than as a relic of the Northern dialect in M. E., where *is* was used throughout the present tense.

SCENE 2

This stirring scene does not yet foreshadow the tragic theme. But it discloses the noble and romantic character of the central figure, known to us hitherto only as a masterful black officer who has run away with a patrician's daughter. Othello's frankness, his quiet dismissal of Iago's would-be politic counsels, his confidence in his integrity ("my perfect soul") no less than in the strength of his position at Venice, convince us that there can, at least, have been nothing mean in his mysterious adventure; while in his union of perfect self-command, instant resource, and repugnance to needless violence, we recognize the finest type of soldier.

6. *'T is better as it is.* "How well these words impress the truth of Othello's character of himself at the end: '(He) was not easily wrought' " (Coleridge).

14. *As double as the duke's,* *i. e.* his single voice weighed as much as the two votes enjoyed by the president of the council. The two votes were a frequent English usage; that the doge of Venice did not, in fact, enjoy them is immaterial.

22. *my demerits,* &c. My deserts entitle me to the rank I hold. The metaphor is from "capping," or doffing the cap (bonnet), to one of superior rank. The word "unbonneted" is loosely formed for "without doffing the cap," bonneted being used (*Coriolanus,* ii. 2, 30) for "took off their caps" (in deference) (cf. Fr. *bonneter,* take off the cap). "Unbonneted" was also a quite idiomatic form for "not wearing a cap," and was so used by Shakespeare himself of the distracted Lear (*King Lear,* iii. 1. 14).

24. *For know,* &c. This touch is our first intimation of the psychical grounds of the marriage, and one of some importance. Othello has lived a joyous, roving, homeless life, free and delighting in freedom; he has surrendered it purely for love of Desdemona.

33. *By Janus.* The oath hints at the ambiguous aspect of the body of officers just at hand, taken for "the raised father and his friends," and proving to be "the servants of the duke" and Cassio. In the only other Shakespearean passage where it is used, *Merchant of Venice,* i. 1. 50 ("Now, by two-headed Janus," &c.), there is a direct allusion to contrasts of character and face:

> "Some that will evermore peep through their eyes
> And laugh like parrots at a bagpiper.
> And other of such vinegar aspect
> That they'll not show their teeth in way of smile,
> Though Nestor swear the jest be laughable."

38. *haste-post-haste* (cf. post-post-haste, i. 3. 46).

53. *Have with you,* take me with you; I'll go with you.

55. *be advised,* consider, take heed.

56. *Holla,* &c.; the exclamation was mostly used as a summons to stop. Cf. "cry holla to thy tongue," *As You Like It,* iii. 2. 257.

59. *Keep . . . rust them.* "One of Shakespeare's miracles" (Bradley). It is our first hint of Othello's brilliant romantic imagination.

67. *So opposite to marriage.* Desdemona, like Othello, has married under the impulse of a sudden attachment, in spite of a pronounced aversion to the married state.

72. *gross in sense,* palpable, too obvious for mistake.

75. *weaken motion,* impair apprehension, and hence sensible action.

SCENE 3

This great scene — a little drama in itself — completes the preliminary action, and puts us in possession of the most important
data of character and incident involved in the tragic sequel. These
are particularly: (1) the characters of Othello and Desdemona themselves, as reflected in their impulsive and romantic marriage; (2) the
animus and aims of Iago, at length frankly disclosed in the final
soliloquy. This passage, it is to be noted, closing the first act, gives
the first hint of the nature of the tragic conflict. The entire first act
is thus devoted to exposition, the only case of this plot-structure in
Shakespeare. At the corresponding point of *Macbeth* we are on the
verge of the crucial moment of the play. Cf. Introduction, § 17.

1. *composition,* accord, consistency. Cf. the use of "disproportioned" (v. 2).

6. *where the aim reports,* where the report is based on a mere
guess.

11. *the main article,* &c., I accept the substance as true, and it
is a terrible truth.

13. *Enter a sailor.* The prompt admission of the sailor to the
sitting of the Grand Council to give his news, emphasizes the extreme urgency of the case.

18. *By no assay of reason,* &c., any reason that may be alleged
for believing it, if tested, will be found idle.

20. *The importancy of Cyprus,* &c. Cyprus was actually taken
by the Turks, in 1570, from the Venetians, who had held it since
1498. The situation represented is that which prevailed at the date
of publication of Cinthio's novel (1555).

23. *more facile question,* easier discussion (struggle).

24. *brace,* state of defense.

25. *abilities, i. e.* warlike equipment.

30. *wake and wage,* rouse and encounter.

44. *Marcus Luccicos,* probably an invented name. The context
suggests that he was meant to be a Cypriot, whose local or other
special knowledge would make him valuable to the expedition.
The imperative summons sent to this foreigner, with "post-post-
haste dispatch," is the counterpart of that sent, demanding his
"haste-post-haste appearance," to the Moorish general, who a moment later appears in answer to it. Othello's employment, we are
to gather, was not a freak but an example of the deliberate Venetian
policy of using the services of foreigners to conduct their campaigns.
"Alwaies they do entertain in honourable sort with great provision

a captain-general, who always is a stranger born'' (Contareno, *Commonwealth of Venice*, tr. Lewkenor, 1599).

62. *For nature . . . could not*, an anacoluthon, or colloquial construction in irregular syntax.

68. *read . . . after your own sense,* interpret as sternly and as literally as you choose.

69. *Stood in,* were the object of, exposed to.

73. This simultaneous exclamation marks the Senate's sense of the dilemma into which the guilt of the indispensable general has brought them.

76. Othello's speech is, with Antony's funeral oration in *Julius Cæsar*, the finest Shakespearean example of natural but finished eloquence. His eloquence is the natural utterance of a man, not subtle or shrewd, but ''holding a volume of force which in repose ensures pre-eminence without an effort'' (Bradley).

95. *her motion blushed at herself,* the impulse which drew her to Othello itself felt shame in the presence of her habitually modest spirit. ''Herself'' is the ''motion'' personified.

104. *To vouch this,* &c. The discovery that the indispensable general is the accused party, enforced by the natural magnetism of his speech and presence, has altered the whole perspective of the case. Othello's speech contains nothing to exculpate him, and even has the air of admitting, in some sense, Brabantio's charges. But it is addressed to men who are now secretly anxious if possible to find him innocent; and the evidence of the ''foul proceeding,'' which at first seemed so convincing that nothing remained but to disclose the culprit, is now slightingly dismissed as ''thin habits and poor likelihoods of modern seeming.''

108. *thin habits . . . seeming,* superficial semblances of guilt based upon mere plausible commonplace. (*Commonplace* is a regular meaning of ''modern.'')

127. *And she in mine.* Othello will not emphasize, but neither will he conceal, the share of Desdemona in effecting their union, as told below. The court must realize that this girl, ''still and quiet'' as her father believed her to be, and as she was, had not been a passive tool in his hands.

This account of Othello's wooing is only intended to meet the charge of ''magic.'' It must be supplemented by Desdemona's account (iii. 3. 70 *f.*) of Cassio's part in it, and the ''many times, when'' he had urged Othello's suit.

142. *It was my hint,* I had occasion. Cf. v. 166 below.

144. *men whose heads,* &c. Cf. *Tempest*, iii. 3. 46 *f*. Gonzalo there mentions those ''men whose heads stood in their breasts'' as a regular topic of travelers' reports, and as hence enjoying some credence, though utterly discredited in his youth.

171. *I think,* &c. Another sign of Othello's power of suggestion. The duke has not *heard* "this tale," but only Othello's summary reference to it.

191. *get,* beget.

195. *for your sake,* on account of your action.

199. *Let me speak like yourself,* as it would become you to speak. The duke's solution — *i. e.* smilingly to accept defeat instead of sullenly nursing the bootless grief — differs only in spirit and temper from Brabantio's, but that is just the difference requisite for "helping these lovers into your favour."

202 f. The rhyme emphasizes the sententious and proverbial character of the duke's argument. At this date Shakespeare hardly used it otherwise, apart from the purely stage device of the final couplet of scenes. See Appendix, Prosody, § II, page 157.

218. *pierced,* penetrated, as if to pour balm into it.

220 f. The abrupt transition to prose marks the consciousness of both men that it is high time to turn from these jingling platitudes to the urgent business of the hour.

230 f. Othello does not love Desdemona less because he returns with "alacrity" (and for an indefinite period) to his soldier's life and work.

232. *thrice-driven,* thrice winnowed, so that only the finest and softest of the down remained.

238. *exhibition,* allowance for maintenance.

250. A bold variation for "my violent taking of my fortune by storm."

251 f. *subdued . . . lord.* Desdemona implies that her inner nature has been colored to her husband's hue. In his 111th Sonnet Shakespeare speaks of his nature as being "subdued to what it works in, like the dyer's hand."

265. *to comply . . . satisfaction.* This reading, though generally adopted, and involving the least change in the text (*me* for Qq Ff. *my*), is far from certain. *Young affects,* passions of youth; *proper,* my own.

267. *defend . . . think,* forbid that you should think.

271. *seel . . . my speculative . . . instruments,* obscure by the clouds of passion the clear perception it is my duty to maintain.

285. Othello's absolute assurance of Iago's "honesty" — an indispensable condition of the coming tragedy — is attested by his choice of him for this responsible trust. And here he was perfectly safe. It is to be remembered that Iago was not, like Cinthio's "ensign," a rejected lover of Desdemona.

290. *delighted,* delightful.

322 ff. An interesting example of Iago's prose, intensely rational and abnormally emotionless.

328. *corrigible.* The terminations *-ible, -able* were still used in an active as well as in a passive sense. So *perdurable* (v. 343). Abbott, § 3.

345. *defeat thy favour,* disguise thy face.

349. *answerable sequestration,* corresponding separation.

352. *luscious as locusts.* Gerarde in his *Herbal* records the belief as then prevalent that the "locusts" of the gospel meant the fruit of the carob tree, a pod full of sweet juice. Shakespeare's usage is probably to be thus understood.

353. *coloquintida,* a bitter fruit used in sixteenth-century medicine.

373. *my cause is hearted, i. e.* my heart is in it.

392. By the word "sport" Iago betrays, what he does not acknowledge even to himself, that the motives he advances for his plot are not those which provide the actual driving power.

399. *plume up,* crown with triumph.

409 f. Furness cites an account of the actor Fechter in this scene: while meditating revenge, he "sits on the angle of the table," "leaning his forehead on his hands, his face hidden," but at "How? how? let's see," he "slowly raises his head and shows his face, which gradually brightens with a diabolical smile." At the last word of the scene he "breaks into a savage, ringing laugh."

ACT II — SCENE 1

The action is now transferred to Cyprus, the scene of the tragedy proper, and the four principal persons concerned in it arrive in succession. Iago's plot is not yet clearly shaped in his mind; but we get further insight into the characters about which he is to weave its deadly meshes, particularly into those dangerous innocences by which they will unconsciously play into his hands. This is facilitated by the separate arrivals. Thus we witness Cassio's enthusiasm for Desdemona, and Desdemona's anxiety for Othello. The culminating moment, their rapturous meeting, makes clear what the first act left open, that their union, however romantic in origin, had called forth in both a deep mutual devotion. It suits Iago's purpose to make light of this to his "poor trash of Venice"; but he sees it clearly himself, and it adds the spice of difficulty to the relish of his game.

9. *hold the mortise, i. e.* not to be disjointed.

15. *guards, i. e.* the stars of the constellation of the Bear.

26. *A Veronesa,* probably a description of the ship as equipped by Verona, one of the Venetian dependencies on the mainland. Qq. Ff. make the word an epithet of Cassio, who has, however, been already described as a Florentine.

38, 39. *Even till . . . regard,* strain our eyes in searching the horizon till the sea and sky seem to meet together. "Indistinct" retains more of the etymological sense, undistinguished, in Shakespearean usage than in ours. Cf. "make it *indistinct,* as water is in water," *Antony and Cleopatra,* iv. 14. 10.

39. *aerial,* pronounced *érial,* and so written in the Folio (Ff. "th' Eriall blew").

43. Cassio's personal devotion to Othello, which goes far beyond the claims of loyalty to a military chief, prepares us for his overwhelming grief at dismissal, and this for Desdemona's compassionate obstinacy in seeking his reinstatement, the one act by which she herself definitely contributes to her fate.

49. *of very . . . allowance,* of well-reputed and tried skill. Cassio's excitement throughout this scene is reflected in the hyperbolical looseness and fervid coloring of his speech. It is the antithesis of the hard, close-packed, grimly logical speech of Iago.

50, 51. *Therefore . . . cure.* Allowing for the traits just adverted to, Cassio may be understood to mean, in substance: "As I left him in danger, I never indulged hopes to the extravagant degree which makes disappointment crushing; and he has a good ship and a tried pilot, so that, in addition, I may confidently look to their fulfilment."

64, 65. *in the essential . . . ingener.* In what nature has made her outdoes what any inventor could contrive.

69. *gutter'd,* indented, hence angular, jagged.

112. *Saints in your injuries,* you do malicious acts with an air of sanctity.

113. *Players in your housewifery,* triflers in the serious business of housekeeping (pronounced *hús(w)ifry*). "Housewife" (husif) was further contracted to "hussy," with the disparaging sense played upon, together with that of "sparing," "grudging," in the following clause.

120. *critical*; always used in Shakespeare of those who pass satirical or censorious judgments. "Some satire, keen and critical" (*Midsummer-Night's Dream,* v. 54). To be "critical" therefore excluded the giving of praise, however well deserved.

121, 122. These lines contain the explanation of the following colloquy with Iago. Desdemona is distracted by anxiety for Othello (cf. her question, v. 120), and seeks this relief.

125. Iago can (cf. v. 118) produce "praise" only by an effort of sheer intellect. The results bear the stamp of his strong, hard wit; but his native cynicism soaks through the barrier of his insincere art and turns these artificial compliments into bitter sarcasms.

147. *put on the vouch,* provoke the acknowledgment.

156. *To change,* &c., to accept the worse in exchange for the better.

161. The utmost merit in a woman qualifies her only to rear babies and keep petty accounts.

166. The courtly Cassio chivalrously excuses Iago's drastic sarcasms: he is a soldier, and this bluntness, which would be bad manners in a scholar, is merely the flavor of his profession.

175, 176. *play the sir in.* Cassio is going beyond the deferential politeness of the lieutenant to his general's wife, to play the courtly gentleman.

177. *clyster-pipes,* tubes used in medical injections. Iago wishes him a disease.

191 f. *If it were now to die,* &c. Othello's thought is at bottom only the sense of the instability of extreme bliss which pre-Aeschylean Greece conveyed in the gross belief that human prosperity provoked the jealousy of the gods, the Middle Ages still more crudely by the myth of Fortune's wheel, and we ourselves by the familiar reflection that "it is too good to last." But Shakespeare has given it in a form original and beautiful, and exquisitely expressive of the vehement but finely-poised passion of the speaker. In Desdemona's rejoinder the different temper of her mind and of her love are beautifully indicated. He is more intense, she more sympathetic. He thinks of the ecstatic moments she has brought him, she of the common and continuous joys of married life.

216 f. *as, they say,* &c. The observation is proverbial. Butler quotes an early example from Plato: "No man is so base that Love himself would not make him of a god-like courage, equal to one most valiant by nature" (*Sympos.* 149). Iago requires Roderigo's help as his tool, and will not yet break with him; but he can insult him to his face with perfect security.

223. *thus, i. e.* to thy lips. In other words, "Listen, and don't talk."

240. *no further conscionable,* &c. Cassio's courtesy (Iago insinuates) is not the expression of an honorable nature, but a mere cloak for his profligate designs.

282, 283. *whose qualification . . . again,* whose tempering or appeasement will only be effected. "Qualify" in Shakespeare is regularly used in this sense; cf. *e. g.* " this inundation of mistempered humour Rests by you only to be qualified" (*King John,* v. 1. 13, &c.).

296. *apt,* natural, and thus easily believed, even if it is not true.

312, 313. *whom I trash For his quick hunting.* Trash is Steevens's emendation for F 1 trace, Q 1 "crush." Trash is a hunting term for a heavy collar used to keep a hound back. "Whom I hold in check for my own purpose from his pursuit of Desdemona." The plot against Cassio was a side-issue, for which Roderigo was to be used. Roderigo himself falls upon the same metaphor below (ii. 3. 370) to describe his situation.

315. *in the rank garb, i. e.* as wanton.

316. *For I fear . . . too.* The character of Iago's plot against Cassio is admirably conveyed by this assertion, as an afterthought, of a possible ground of quarrel with him. This defense had not occurred to him when originally conceiving his plot (*i.* 3. 398 *f.*).

SCENE 2

9. *offices,* the service-quarters of the house, hence especially the stores of food and drink. Cf. "all our offices have been oppress'd with riotous feeders" (*Timon of Athens*, ii. 1. 167).

SCENE 3

This important scene opens Iago's intrigue, and shows the first step in it, the disgrace of Cassio, carried out with complete success. Othello, Cassio, Roderigo, Montano are all his dupes, but his action and counsel are so speciously "honest," and in part so undeniably sound, that no loop-hole is left open, as yet, even for suspicion. He acts perfectly the part of a boon companion in making Cassio drunk, that of a kindly but responsible officer in reporting to his chief, that of a shrewd and sympathetic comrade in counselling his victim how to proceed in seeking redress.

31. *a brace.* They are in fact three (v. 57 below).

32. *a measure, i. e.* of wine; the "stoup" (2 quarts) just mentioned.

41. *craftily qualified,* prudently diluted.

42. *innovation.* In Elizabethan English, regularly a change for the worse.

58. *That hold . . . distance,* that resent the least approach to insult, easily provoked to quarrel.

91 f. A stanza from a ballad preserved in the *Percy Folio MS.,* and published in the *Reliques.* The king is there "Henry." King Stephen's breeches "that cost him but a crown" were a stock Elizabethan allusion.

104. Cassio's honorable instincts sound a muffled call in his obfuscated brain, but are not wholly suppressed. Cf. v. 116.

127. It was by speciously fair judgments of this kind that Iago won his reputation for "honesty." Cf. v. 147 *f.*

136. *He'll watch,* &c., *i. e.* two circuits of the clock-hand, twenty-four hours.

170. *turned Turks.* Othello plays bitterly upon the phrase, which was used proverbially of a change for the worse. The change here in question was precluded for the Turks by their Mohammedan law.

175. *dreadful.* The precise shade of meaning is given by the next clause. Cf. v. 214.

185. *peevish odds,* idle quarrel, one begun on a trifling provocation.

188. *Michael.* This intimate address, marking Othello's affectionate confidence in the lieutenant whom he had preferred even to "honest Iago," is here used for the last time. When cashiered, though Othello still "loves" him, he becomes and remains "Cassio."

216. *on the . . . safety,* a mixture of the phrases "court of guard" (main guard-house) and "guard of safety." Othello, in his rising passion, exasperated that the very place appointed to maintain order should have been the scene of a dangerous disturbance, uses language clear to the sense rather than to grammar.

218. *partially affined,* made partial by any tie. Montano suspects that Iago may try to shield his brother officer.

231 *f.* Iago artfully plays upon the anxiety which Othello has already expressed.

273. *in his mood,* in a fit of anger. Cf. *e. g.* "who in my mood I stabb'd unto the heart" (*Two Gentlemen of Verona,* iv. 1. 51). For *cast* see Glossary.

280. *speak parrot.* Cf. for the construction, "he speaks nothing but madman" (*Twelfth Night,* i. 5, 115).

347. *fruitful,* &c., generous, giving without stint.

355. *parallel, i. e.* corresponding to my arrangement.

358. *suggest,* tempt.

392. *jump,* just, at the very moment.

ACT III — SCENE 1

This short scene brings us several steps nearer to the "solicitation" of Desdemona by Cassio on which Iago, as the last lines of Act ii. indicate, relies for the first suggestion of suspicion. Emilia and Desdemona, it seems, as well as Othello himself (v. 51), are anxious for Cassio's restoration, which would clearly have come about after an interval. It is a part of Iago's good luck that Cassio, tortured by his disgrace, cannot wait the event, but invokes Desdemona's intercession on the very morning after the brawl. His provision of music, played with morning greetings, as was usual, under the windows of the bridal chamber, was itself a tacit appeal to Othello's clemency, an appeal which Othello, suspecting its origin, peremptorily rejects. For the clown, see Introduction, p. xxxvi.

42. Cassio, himself a Florentine, finds Iago's "kind and honest" demeanor worthy of his own countrymen. It naturally impresses him the more, since Desdemona's appeal, which Iago was furthering, would if successful destroy his prospect of succeeding to Cassio's coveted post. The Venetians were proverbially crafty. The reputed "cunning" of Venetian women made it easier to break down Othello's faith in the exceptional purity of Desdemona. Cf. iv. 2. 88.

43. Emilia shows her good-natured sympathy with Cassio by giving him his forfeited title.

45. *your displeasure, i. e.* the disfavor you have incurred.

47. *she speaks for you stoutly.* We are to suppose that Emilia has already "moved her mistress" in this sense; but Desdemona's friendly disposition towards Cassio would make her action natural in any case.

52. *To take . . . front.* Compare "take time by the forelock," a parallel version of the same saying.

SCENE 3

This, commonly called the "temptation scene," consists in reality of six scenes.

(1) *Desdemona and Cassio* (1–34). Desdemona, led by Emilia's persuasion and her chivalrous interest in Cassio, assures him of her advocacy with engaging but dangerous frankness. Othello and Iago approaching at the moment when she is imploring him to stay, Iago promptly makes use of the opening thus provided.

(2) *Desdemona's first pleading with Othello* (41–92). Othello is clearly irritated by Cassio's importunity. Desdemona he does not yet dream of suspecting, but he is justly irritated by the impolitic urgency with which she tries to bind him to a time, and finally dismisses her with an impatience hardly concealed by its courteous form.

(3) *Iago's first colloquy with Othello* (92–276). Iago now begins to exploit with extraordinary skill the materials so far available against Cassio, and circumspectly to suggest Desdemona's complicity. His dark hints of something which he is resolved not to betray intimate that his secret touches Othello more nearly than

any fault of Cassio alone. Presently he warns Othello against jealousy, and insinuates the word "cuckold." All this acting upon Othello's nature with maddening effect, Iago can now, with an air of reluctant submission, note the possible grounds for suspicion against Desdemona.

(4) *Othello and Desdemona* (279–289). The dropping of the handkerchief which is to provide Iago with his deadliest shaft; a pure accident, a part of his fabulous good luck.

(5) *Emilia and Iago* (290–329). Iago, with hardly concealed joy, takes possession of the handkerchief.

(6) *Iago's second colloquy with Othello* (330–end). The poison has now entered Othello's soul. On his demanding ocular proof, Iago adduces two pieces of evidence, Cassio's dream, and his possession of Desdemona's handkerchief. The latter being apparently substantiated, Othello is convinced; in a sublime poetic image, he declares that his purpose of revenge is fixed, and Iago, who has all styles at his command, simulates his exaltation.

23. *Watch him tame,* as hawks were tamed by being kept from sleep.

51. *call him back, i. e.* replace him in office.

66. *Out of their best, i. e.* even of the best warriors.

not . . . check, hardly deserving so much as a private reprimand.

91. *and when I love thee not . . . again,* a vivid Elizabethan way of saying "should I not love thee, chaos would come again." His words express a nature so completely penetrated and possessed by the exaltation of love that it would fall to pieces should love be withdrawn.

122. *tricks of custom,* conventional phrases.

123. *close delations,* &c., secret disclosures of the truth issuing from a heart unswayed by passion.

127. *those that be not,* &c., I wish that those that are not what they seem would not seem what they are not.

129. Iago uses the distinction just drawn between seeming and being to give an equivocal testimony to Cassio's honesty. He "thinks" him honest, that is, he "seems" honest, but that is no guarantee that he is.

131. *as to thy thinkings,* with as little reserve as to thy own thoughts.

134. *free to, i. e.* free to refuse.

138 f. In the purest breast suspicions of guilt have their legitimate place, and sit in judgment upon the supposed culprits with reflections under these conditions lawful. *Leets* were district-courts held half-yearly for the trial of non-capital offences.

151. *scattering,* straggling.

166. *green-eyed . . . mock.* Some modern editors have thought it necessary to change "mock" to "make"; but the text as it stands was well explained by Hunter: "Jealousy mocks the person who surrenders his mind to her influence . . . sporting herself with his agonized feelings, just as the feline tribe sport with the prey which they have got into their power."

167. *that cuckold,* &c., *i. e.* the betrayed husband, who already knows the worst, and has withdrawn his love from the faithless wife, is happy in comparison with one who is tormented by doubt, and fears without being able to resign his love.

182. *exsufflicate and blown,* swollen, as with air; windy, idle.

206. Iago almost verbally repeats Brabantio's parting shaft. The effect, for Othello, is to add the authority of her father's evidence to the presumption of her guilt.

225. *honest,* chaste (as commonly).

250. *strain his entertainment, i. e.* urge his restoration to favor.

260 f. *If I do prove her . . . fortune.* If I find her untameable (false to her wifely duty), I will sever the ties that bind us, though I should rend my heart to do it, and cast her loose to seek adventures at will. The *haggard,* in falconry, was a wild, untameable hawk; the *jesses,* thongs of leather bound to the hawk's legs, by which it was secured.

276. *this forked plague, i. e.* a wife's infidelity, symbolized by the thorns.

283. Othello plays grimly upon the idea indicated in the last note. Desdemona, with an innocence which might have disarmed the suspicion, as her appearance so nearly does, takes the words literally.

288. The stage direction here is modern.

296. *ta'en out,* copied.

312. *to the advantage,* availing myself of the favorable opportunity.

318. *Be not acknown on it,* do not admit your knowledge of it.

328. *I did say so.* Othello's face bears witness to the inner torment which Iago has just described.

330. *mandragora,* a narcotic made of the mandrake root.

385. *I think . . . is not.* Othello thinks, or believes he thinks, two opposite thoughts at once; one to which he still desperately clings in spite of the facts, and one to which the facts have all but forced his assent. The subjunctive *be,* so far as it has any effect, suggests that the first statement is less assured.

428. *a foregone conclusion,* something already accomplished.

453. *Like to the Pontic sea,* &c. The image, turned into high poetry by the passion of Othello, is taken almost unaltered from the matter-of-fact description of Pliny, as translated by Philemon Holland (1601): "And the sea Pontus evermore floweth and runneth out into Propontis, but the sea never retireth back again within Pontus."

SCENE 4

The two lines of Iago's plot — Cassio's disgrace leading to Desdemona's pleading for his reinstatement, and the suspicious disappearance of the handkerchief leading to Othello's fierce demand for it — now meet in a focus of unsurpassed dramatic intensity. The impetuous resolve of Othello to have assurance of the worst, and Desdemona's chivalrous importunity, concur with deadly effect. Her doom is now sealed.

16. The clown's "catechize" carries on the allusion suggested by Desdemona's "edified."

26. *cruzadoes,* a Portuguese gold coin.

38. *fruitfulness and liberal heart,* generosity; but with a covert allusion to the other senses of fruitfulness (fertility) and liberal (licentious).

40. *sequester,* sequestration, removal.

74. *mummy,* the juice of mummies used for magical purposes. In *Macbeth,* iv. 1. 23, "witches' mummy" is one of the ingredients of the cauldron. Here the juice is specifically derived from maidens' hearts.

99. *the happiness! i. e.* happily encountered.

108. Emilia finds her belief in Othello's jealousy (v. 30) confirmed. It has been rightly thought incredible that Emilia, at this point, should not recollect the incident of the handkerchief's loss. Her promptness in putting the topic aside, itself indicates that she is only suppressing what she knows. To tell what she knew would have been to disclose that it was in Iago's hands, and to provoke his instant wrath. But she does not until the disclosure scene even suspect a connection between his borrowing of the handkerchief and its provocation of this "jealousy" in Othello.

119. *But to know,* merely to know.

128. *within the blank,* &c., exposed to its full brunt (as the bull's eye of the target).

134. *I have seen the cannon,* &c. Iago's style is habitually compressed and often, as here, elliptical. He leaves it to be understood that Othello has suffered these losses unmoved.

141. *some unhatched practice,* &c., a plot discovered before it was ripe for execution.

149. *look for such observances,* &c., the punctilious respect, natural at a burial ceremony.

151. *unhandsome warrior,* &c., a poor soldier, unworthy to accompany any husband to camp.

156. *jealous toy,* idle suspicion.

173. *a week away.* See Appendix II.

180. *Take . . . out.* See iii. 3. 296.

182. *to the felt absence,* &c., *i. e.* in addition to the pain of Cassio's absence she now suffers from the cause she imputes it to.

194. *addition,* honor.

198. *soon at night,* after nightfall.

201. *I must be circumstanced,* I must comply with circumstances, put up with things as they are.

ACT IV — SCENE 1

Iago's strategy in this final phase of his deadly game has two phases. In the first he forces Othello to face the full import of the two strong points already made — Cassio's "confession" and the loss of the handkerchief — with the result that Othello falls in a trance. Then he clinches the effect with his most audacious device — his overheard conversation with Cassio. Only a mind saturated, as Othello's is, and as Iago knows that it is, with the "poison," could be gulled by so gross an imposture. Desdemona's death was already decided. He now gives definite orders for "poison" — recalled, at Iago's sinister suggestion (he is an artist in crime), in favor of the more "pleasing justice" of death by strangling. But the tragic climax is the blow — provoked by her innocently frank professions of "love" for Cassio, and joy (as he takes her to mean) in his promotion. The purpose of this otherwise not very clearly motived arrival of Lodovico from Venice at this point is that she may express in Othello's presence her naïve desire to "atone" them.

6. *i. e.* they feign sin to delude the devil.

40 f. It cannot be for nothing that I feel a passion so full of imagined shapes (the confused vision of the "handkerchief" and the "confessions" evoked by Iago). Mere "words" might be illusory. On the use of prose here, see Appendix I, pp. 154–55.

42. *noses, ears, and lips,* half inarticulate ejaculations called forth by the image of the lovers' supposed familiarities reflected in his tortured and now ebbing consciousness.

61. *Dost thou mock me?* He suspects an allusion to "horns."

69 f. *unproper,* which they share unwittingly with others. *peculiar,* solely their own.

72. *secure,* free from fear of rivalry.

76. *in a patient list,* in the bounds of patience.

82. *encave, i. e.* hide.

102. *unbookish,* uninstructed.

122. *customer,* wanton woman.

130. *Have you scored me?* have you made my reckoning, *i. e.*
settled accounts with me as Desdemona's actual husband.

150. *before me,* an exclamation of surprise — "God possess me!"

218. *unprovide,* throw into disorder.

248. Desdemona thinks of Othello's recall only as a joyful and
triumphant return home; he, knowing that he is in reality cashiered,
supposes her to be "glad" at the honor conferred on Cassio and his
own humiliation. After the blow, not knowing how otherwise to
explain it, she supposes that after all he must be displeased by his
recall. Hence her helpless attempt below (ii. 34–5) to soothe him.

256. *teem with,* be made pregnant by.

257. *falls,* lets fall.

SCENE 2

Othello's infatuation, wrought step by step to the point of agonized but undoubting conviction, has so far been carefully guarded
by Iago from contact with those who had a clue to the truth. Cassio,
the most dangerous of all, after being used to clinch the deceit, is
to be put out of the way (iv. 1. 224). Emilia, on the contrary, who
was destined to ruin his calculations, though not in time to save
her mistress, gives him no concern. This is *his* infatuation, like
Macbeth's faith in the stability of Birnam wood. He despised her
too completely to take precautions on her account, and till the
close, with good ground. She has already witnessed Othello's
"jealousy": she is now for the first time directly confronted by it.
She bears witness warmly and indignantly to her mistress's innocence, but Othello is now impervious to evidence, even had hers not
been impaired by her dubious reputation (v. 21–3). Scorning Emilia's
plea, he now in the wonderful passage which follows — half-bitter,
quasi-judicial questioning, half-rapt ejaculations of a soul struggling
in agony — brings the charge for the first time directly home to his
wife. Loathing and inextinguishable passions contend in him, as
foulness and heavenly beauty mingle, he thinks, in her.

Then we are shown the effect of this overwhelming blow upon her
uncomprehending, innocent, but rather helpless soul. It leaves her
at first dazed and almost speechless. And it is not to Emilia, with
her warm indignation, but to "good" Iago, with his crocodile pity,

that she turns confidently for help; a stroke of Shakespearean irony which greatly enhances the pathos.

Iago's final passage with Roderigo belongs only outwardly to this scene. If driven to bay, even Roderigo might harm Iago's credit by betraying his part in the pursuit of Desdemona. Iago's skilful *coup* disposes of him and Cassio — either or both — at the same time.

3. *she.* The substitution of the nominative for the accusative is common in Elizabethan and later English after *and; e. g.* "All debts are cleared between you and I" (*Merchant of Venice*, iii. 2. 318).

28. *Some of your function;* pertaining to Emilia in the character alluded to in vv. 20 *f.* Believing his wife to be unfaithful, he bitterly treats her as an inmate, and Emilia as the keeper, of a house of ill-fame. Hence the allusion to her "mystery" (calling), v. 30, and the ironical offer of "payment," v. 93.

54 *f.* A disputed passage. The imagery seems to represent Othello as standing motionless while the concentrated scorn of his age points him out relentlessly. The reading "slow unmoving" is that of Q, but the F reading, "slow and moving," may be right — the equivalent of "slowly moving"; in that case the finger of time is thought of as moving like the hand of a clock.

72. *committed.* Desdemona had used the word in the general sense as applied to any fault; Othello takes it in the special sense as applied to adultery. Cf. "Commit not with man's sworn spouse" (*King Lear*, iii. 4. 48).

77. *winks,* closes her eye.

104. *go by water, i. e.* be uttered with tears.

107. This line is probably addressed to Emilia; the two following are soliloquy. Hence the "Exit" might better be indicated after 107.

130. *eternal.* The word was used as an epithet of vague abuse, like our "infernal." So "the eternal devil" (*Julius Cæsar*, i. 2. 160).

132. *to get some office.* In spite of this phrase it must not be supposed that Emilia is covertly hinting that her husband is the "man." She does not yet suspect him, as is shown by her amazed iteration at v. 2. 146 *f.*

144. *Speak within door,* with the sarcastic suggestion that her vehement outburst will be heard in the street.

146 *f.* This reduces to its true dimensions Iago's calumnious suggestion at i. 3. 393.

SCENE 3

The scene adds little or nothing to the progress of the action — merely Othello's curt order to his wife to go to bed and dismiss Emilia, and her unquestioning compliance. But it adds material traits to the portraits of both women. Desdemona, stunned by the consciousness that Othello has ceased to love her, has lost all trace of the girlish spirit which had provoked her brave intervention for Cassio. It had served her ill then; but a question to Emilia about the handkerchief might now have brought out the truth in time to save her. As it is, she goes helplessly to her doom. Her colloquy with Emilia shows that it proceeds from a purity of soul so absolute that it cannot entertain the thought of infidelity under whatever provocation; while Emilia's knowledge of the world is seen to go with the vulgar conception of wedded fidelity as a bargain, binding on the wife only so long as the husband observes it. Dr. Bradley points out the frequency in Shakespearean tragedy of a scene, like this, of tender and pathetic beauty, shortly before the catastrophe. So the meeting of Lear and Cordelia (iv. 7), the talk of Lady Macduff with her little son (iv. 2), the madness of Ophelia (iv. 5).

27. *mad,* wild, wanton; and hence faithless.

31, 32. *I have much to do, but,* &c., I can hardly refrain from, &c.

41. A ballad very similar to this of Desdemona's is to be found in the Pepys collection at Oxford; and music for it occurs in a lute book of 1583; the setting is reproduced in Furness's New Variorum edition, p. 278.

52. *Let nobody,* &c. This line, so perfectly expressive of Desdemona's own feeling, comes to her mind, by sheer force of aptness, out of its context; an exquisite trait.

73. *joint ring,* a ring with joints.

75. *exhibition,* allowance.

84. *to the vantage,* to boot.

88 f. The change to verse here indicates the transition to a more serious mood. Emilia now puts forward what she regards as the real excuse for the infidelity of wives.

92. *having,* allowance.

ACT V — SCENE 1

A scene of action. The critical moment in Iago's affairs ("the night that either makes me or fordoes me quite") is come. Roderigo can no longer be deluded; Cassio, too, is a standing peril to the success of his plot. Both, therefore, he now decides, must die; the attack already arranged is likely to dispose of one at least; Iago privately resolves to complete the work, and (as in the drinking scene in Act ii) to win fresh credit for his "honest" and loyal intervention. It is a very dark night (v. 42) and identities are at fault. With one exception his calculations succeed. Cassio is not mortally

wounded, and will later clinch the demonstration of Iago's guilt
(v. 2. 299 f.).

1. *this bulk,* some projecting part of the (timber) houses in the
street.

14. *Live Roderigo.* The construction of a conditional sentence
with the subjunctive of the simple verb was still current in Elizabethan
English (Modern English: "should Roderigo live"). Cf. "Prove this
a prosperous day, the three-nook'd world Shall bear the olive freely"
(*Antony and Cleopatra,* iv. 6. 6).

29. Othello's first words (v. 28), as he entered in the darkness,
expressed only a strong surmise, which he now, and again at v. 31
(" 'T is he"), finds confirmed.

37. *no passage?* are there no people about?

42. *heavy,* dark, and thus favorable to treachery such as Lodovico
suspects.

47. *cries on murder,* cries "Murder!" as for help.

106. *gastness,* expression of horror. Bianca loves Cassio in her
fashion, and is genuinely terrified for his safety. Iago uses her
"stare" as a presumption of her guilt.

SCENE 2

The comprehensive closing scene opens with the catastrophe of
the tragic action, followed, with the most rigorous dramatic sequence,
by the discovery, the flight, and arrest of Iago, and the death of
Othello.

The transitions in Othello's mood up to the moment of the murder
are marked with wonderful delicacy. His resolution has been taken,
and does not for a moment flag; if anguish forces tears from him as
he watches her asleep, they are "cruel tears," which will not arrest the
stroke. When she wakes and speaks, he recovers self-possession,
putting his brief, ominous questions with a forced calm more terrible
than violence, yet betraying increasing inward agitation in the
movement of his eyes and lips. Her naïve declaration that all her
"sin" was love for him does not touch him. But when she meets his
direct charge with eager denial, his patience gives way, his heart
grows "stony," and the "ill-starred" words in which she seems to
grieve that her guilt and Cassio's is discovered, precipitate her doom.

The knocking of Emilia (distantly paralleled by the knocking at
the castle gates in *Macbeth*) preludes the discovery. Her splendid
defiance, first of Othello, then of her husband, is the great feature
of the following section of the scene. Iago's masterful game is
completely checkmated by this attack from the one quarter he

thought secure, and, with the fatuity which even an able criminal will often display in such a situation, he gives himself away by futile violence and futile flight. Cassio's explanation of the letters of Roderigo leaves the case completely clear.

Othello's assaults upon Iago are momentary impulses, consciously futile. Finally, when about to end all, he rises to a height of clear judgment upon himself, with the penetrating insight which calamity brings to the least introspective of Shakespeare's tragic heroes.

1. *It is the cause,* &c. Othello steels himself to his deed — to which the sight of her innocent beauty gives new poignancy — by fastening on the thought that he is the instrument of offended justice.

18, 19. *Be thus . . . and love thee after,* *i. e.* be thus . . . and I will love thee after, notwithstanding that I shall have caused thy death.

40. *They are loves I bear to you.* She thinks of her deception of her father, for what else can he mean?

52. *presently,* immediately, in a moment (not "after an interval").

61. *love.* The word could then denote a merely kindly feeling such as Desdemona might properly entertain for Cassio.

63 *f. stone,* petrify. Desdemona's "infidelity" caused Othello rather anguish than hate; her "perjury" rouses his indignation, and he will now kill her because he desires her blood, not as an offering which he is bound to make.

72. *ta'en order,* given orders, taken measures.

76. Desdemona means that Cassio, who could have vindicated her innocence and his own, has been treacherously slain, involving her in ruin.

82. *Being done,* &c., all being now irrevocably settled, there is no further respite.

88. *So, so.* At these words, according to an old stage tradition, Othello stabs Desdemona, completing the work begun by stifling her; but there is no warrant for this in the text. On the situation which permits Desdemona to speak audibly after having been strangled, Furness consulted several distinguished surgeons; see their replies in the New Variorum edition, pp. 302–307. One of them, Dr. William Hunt, stated that if we assume that Othello broke the cricoid cartilege of Desdemona's larynx the details that follow are "exactly in accordance with the ordinary sequence of symptoms."

101. *yawn at alteration,* gape or burst open as with horror at the change. On this passage Bradley comments: "A blackness suddenly intervenes between his eyes and the world; he takes it for the shuddering testimony of nature to the horror he has just heard." (*Shake-spearean Tragedy*, p. 196.)

107. *What, now?* Othello starts at the unintended aptness of the words.

109. *the very error of the moon.* The moon has swung from her appointed path into the neighborhood of the earth, so that her "stroke," which produces "lunacy," is more deadly.

129. *She's, like a liar, gone,* &c. The words revolt us, and have been thought "unlike Othello," in the sense of being untrue to his character. But in these first moments he is completely unmanned; his mind reels, and this savage phrase may be regarded as equivalent to a violent oath, repudiating his denial of guilt just before in an access of fierce sincerity.

144. *such another, i. e.* as this world.

151. *hath made mocks with love,* has made sport with, deluded, tricked Othello's love for his wife.

157. *filthy,* in allusion to Othello's color.

177. *apt,* natural, easily accounted for (cf. ii. 1. 296).

220. *liberal,* without restraint or regard.

239. *notorious,* see Glossary. Iago was universally reputed "honest." His villainy, "notorious" enough in the Elizabethan sense, was only now discovered.

253. *the ice-brook's temper.* Spanish swords were said to be tempered by being plunged, straight from the forge, in an ice-cold brook.

268. *sea-mark,* a mark or beacon set up for the guidance of ships; hence goal or terminus.

287. *a fable.* That the devil's feet were cloven.

299. *Dear general,* &c. "One is sure Cassio had never used that adjective before. . . . It tells us that his hero is no longer unapproachably above him" (Bradley).

314. *another discontented paper,* the ground of the "discontent" appearing below, v. 323 *f.*

338–359. "As he speaks these final words in which all the glory and agony of his life . . . seem to pass before us, like the pictures that flash before the eyes of a drowning man, a triumphant scorn for the fetters of the flesh and the littleness of all the lives that must survive him sweeps our grief away, and when he dies upon a kiss, the most painful of tragedies leaves us for the moment free from pain, and exulting in the power of 'love and man's unconquerable mind.'" (Bradley: *Shakespearean Tragedy*, p. 198.)

339. Othello recalls his services merely to get a hearing after the order has been given. But he will not have it imagined that he means to claim any remission of punishment on that score; hence brushes the matter immediately aside.

347. *the base Indian.* No incident is known to which this can be thought to refer directly, but ignorance of the value of jewels, on the part of savages, seems to have been a familiar theme. The F text reads "Judean," which some editors prefer, believing that Othello compares himself with Judas.

353. *turban'd.* The turban conveyed to the Elizabethans suggestions of ferocity and paganism. Cf. "giants may get through and keep their impious turbans on" (*Cymbeline*, iii. 3. 6).

371. *this heavy act,* the whole tragic story.

APPENDIX I

PROSODY

SUMMARY

I. VERSE AND PROSE

1. Contrary to classical and other foreign precedent, Shakespeare, like most of his contemporaries and successors, mingled verse and prose in the same play, in the same scene, and even in the same speech.

2. Up to about 1597 the distribution between them which prevails later in his work is not yet established. The influence of Marlowe in particular made for the uniform use of verse; this is almost exclusively used in the early Histories, while in the later (*1* and *2 Henry IV* and *Henry V*) about half is prose. It may be taken as certain that had *King John* (*e.g.*) been written in 1599 the earlier speeches of Falconbridge would have been prose. From about 1597 onward the distribution is guided by certain principles, which can in general be recognized. The precise explanation of particular passages is often doubtful. But it is important to realize that the use of prose and verse is never arbitrary.

3. These principles may be stated thus: *Verse* is used, normally, (*a*) to emphasize *passion*, in situation or in character. It accompanies a heightened emotional temperature, and often marks the sudden passage of a scene into this heightened mood. Thus, when the funeral procession, headed by the king and queen, approaches

the graveyard at Elsinore, Hamlet and Horatio break off their prose
colloquy upon the dust of Alexander with:

> But soft! but soft! aside: here comes the king.
>
> *(Hamlet,* v. 1. 240.)

So, without any such outer provocation, Volumnia's exultation in
her son suddenly breaks through the sober vesture of prose into lyric:

These are the ushers of Marcius: before him he carries noise, and
behind him he leaves tears:

> Death, that dark spirit, in 's nervy arm doth lie,
> Which, being advanced, declines, and then men die.
>
> *(Coriolanus,* ii. 1. 171 *f.)*

(*b*) Though this principle is less consistently applied, verse is
recognized as *nobler,* and therefore more appropriate to high-born
persons; and as these, in Shakespeare, habitually play the leading
part in the action, the framework of the plot and the crucial scenes
are normally in verse. Verse may hence also mark the ceremonial
or deferential language of subordinate or low-class characters. It may
also be the medium of quite prosaic and matter-of-fact statements
by noble persons, *e.g.* the archbishop's justification of the king's
title (*Henry V,* i. 2. 32 *f.*), one of the flattest passages in Shakespeare.

Naturally these "principles" are not consistent, and frequently
interfere with one another in practice. The one reflects the sensitive literary instinct of Shakespeare the poet, the other the aristo-
cratic prejudices of Shakespeare the man.

4. In the absence of either of these motives for verse, prose is
normal. Clearly this may arise from several distinct causes. Thus
prose is the normal medium of (*a*) *low-class* characters: the *ple-
beians* at Rome (*Julius Cæsar, Coriolanus*); sailors (*Tempest, Hamlet*);
Trinculo and Stephano (*Tempest*); the players and gravediggers
(*Hamlet*); while in the immature Histories the citizens (*Richard III*)
and the gardeners (*Richard II*) speak blank verse.

But when low-class characters have passion and pathos, like the
murderers in *Macbeth,* they use verse. And note that Caliban,
though treated as a slave by Prospero, speaks only in *verse,* a significant hint that this scion of the unspoilt new world is after all
less ignoble than the dregs of civilization with whom he conspires.

(*b*) *Comic* situations and characters. This often concurs with
(*a*) as in the porter (*Macbeth*), the gravediggers (*Hamlet*), Dogberry
and Verges, and most of the *clowns* and *jesters.* But Falstaff, though

well-born, also speaks exclusively prose, except when he is parodying the "noble" manner of the stage-court (*1 Henry IV*, 4. 431).

(*c*) Sardonic, cynical, sarcastic characters, moods, and situations: *e.g.* Don John (*Much Ado*), Lucio (*Measure for Measure*), and the patrician Menenius (*Coriolanus*); so most of the bitter colloquies of Hamlet; while in his soliloquies bitterness is lifted into passion.

(*d*) Matter-of-fact, dryly "realistic," "prosaic" characters, moods, situations. Thus documents and letters, when quoted; *e.g.* Macbeth's (*Macbeth*, i. 5), Posthumus's (*Cymbeline*, iii. 2, iv. 4).

(*e*) Distinct from these is the use of prose for the incoherent language of *madness* (Lear, Edgar, Ophelia), frenzy, or mental paralysis.

5. But these various motives for prose or verse rarely occur singly. They are therefore often in conflict, and the decision in favor of one or the other is a means of delicate dramatic effect. Thus the most romantic and noble persons habitually speak prose with the Clown; and Falstaff's powerful magnetism creates prose wherever he moves. Hamlet speaks prose not only when he is sarcastic, but in his first cordial welcome to, or, later, in earnest expostulation with, the insignificant Rosencrantz and Guildenstern.

6. We may now apply these general laws of Shakespearean prose and verse to the present play. Taking the characters separately:

OTHELLO and DESDEMONA speak normally in verse. But Othello's mental "chaos" (iv. 1. 34*f.*, 180*f.*) is given in prose (4 *e*), and Desdemona, forcing her mood to playfulness in ii. 1. 122*f.*, speaks prose to Iago (5), while he, forcing his mood no less, in converse with his general's lady, speaks particularly stilted verse. Contrast her pleading colloquy with him in iv. 2. 110*f.*, where she is deeply in earnest and wholly herself. Othello's prose speech of directions to his wife (iv. 1. 7*f.*) may be meant to emphasize the rigid formality of the words. He no longer abuses her in public ("looks gentler than he did"), but he will not use the language of affection.

IAGO, on the contrary, speaks naturally and normally *prose* (4 *c*, *d*). But throughout the play he is playing a part. Hence with Othello and Desdemona he habitually speaks verse (5); it is a sign of his conscious superiority to his credulous victim in the fourth act that, when Othello ceases to use verse (the prose of frenzy), Iago adopts with him, too, prose. His nominal subordination is cancelled. With superior persons in general (cf. the transition to verse when he addresses Montano in the brawl scene, ii. 3. 123), while in familiar talk with Cassio, in the same scene, and almost throughout with Roderigo, whom he despises, he talks prose. But this cynic has one subject of exaltation—his plot; hence the soliloquies which show him hatching the successive steps, or exulting in their success, are in verse (i. 3. 389 f.; ii. 1. 294 f.; ii. 3. 50 and 342 f.; iii. 3. 320 f., 389 f.; v. 1. 11 f.). With Roderigo, in the opening scene, he is not yet on familiar terms (cf. his "sir" and "you," afterwards always "thou"), and uses the more ceremonial language. In ii. 375 f. the exultation of having won the first decisive move in his game, reflected in the preceding and following soliloquies, still animates him ("does 't not go well?"). In v. 1. 1 f. his few lines of verse to Roderigo may be taken to mark the excitement of the critical moment ("it makes us or it mars us"). With Brabantio (i. 1. 80 f.) he is at first assuming the language of "terrible summons," and verse goes well with such un-Iagolike lyrical turns as "Awake; what ho!"—"Even now, now, very now"—"Arise, arise." In 108 f., provoked to plain speaking, even with a magnifico of Venice, he reverts to his native prose. The matter of this passage and of 86 f. is much the same; but he was there professedly announcing a monstrous piece of news, here he is merely expostulating.

RODERIGO's use of verse and prose is here sufficiently characterized.

CASSIO, a naturally lyrical character, speaks verse habitually, except in familiar talk with Iago (ii. 3. 11 f.; iv. 1. 111 f.), in the drinking bout, and in the contemptuous dismissal of Bianca (ib. 152 f.). His prose in the anguished colloquy with Iago which follows (ii. 3. 260 f.) may be explained by the obsession of the prose-character of Iago (5). Had his cry, "O, I have lost my reputation! I have lost the immortal part of myself . . .," been uttered in soliloquy, it would probably have been in verse.

EMILIA is seen only in company with persons with whom she is on deferential terms, her mistress, her master, and her husband. She falls into prose only once, in the cynical confession of her last confidential talk with Desdemona (iv. 3. 70 f.).

BIANCA, by class and character, may be expected to speak prose (4 a). And this is the natural medium for her vulgar abuse of Cassio, iv. 1. 152 (4 c). Contrast with this her wistful pleading with him (iii. 4. 169 f.), appropriately in verse.

The CLOWN, as usual, speaks prose throughout (ii. 1.; iii. 4). And, as is equally usual, his mistress conforms to him. So Cassio, iii. 1. 22 f. Cf. Lear's prose speeches to his Fool in the midst of his passionate verse. The conventional condescension to the Fool, as to a quasi-equal, is thus effectually symbolized.

SAILOR. The sailor who is ushered into the presence of the Venetian Senate (i. 3) would normally speak prose (4 a), but uses the more ceremonial language in deference (5).

HERALD. The proclamation (ii. 2) is in prose (4 d).

The Duke and other Venetian patricians regularly use verse.

There is one exception only, the speeches in which Brabantio and the Duke turn from the affair of Othello's marriage to the proper and urgent business of the meeting (i. 3. 220-9). This may be best considered a case of 4 d. The transition from the high-flown "sentences" of the two grandees to the crying "facts" of the moment is effectively marked by the nakedly prosaic form of the speech in which the Duke complies with Brabantio's appeal:

> "I humbly beseech you, proceed to the affairs of state."

II. RHYME

At the date of Othello, Shakespeare had long ceased to admit rhyme simply as a beautiful variation on blank verse, as he does in the *Midsummer-Night's Dream* and in *Richard II*. But he had not yet come to confine it to the single function which it retains in the latest plays as the final couplet of a scene. In the present play it is used to heighten the effect of a string of sententious epigrams, as in the Duke's plea with Brabantio, and Brabantio's sarcastic retort (i. 3. 202-19). Similarly, it adds to the effect of artifice in Iago's "praise" of Desdemona, which comes from his brain "as birdlime does from frize" (ii. 1. 130 f.) and to occasional epigrammatic or sententious turns of his elsewhere (as iii. 3. 379-80). So in Othello's bitter epigram (v. 1. 35-6).

III. SCANSION

1. ELIZABETHAN PRONUNCIATION

(1) The current pronunciation of English in Elizabethan times differed widely from ours, and some of the differences affect the proper scansion of their verse. Thus (1) the *accent* sometimes fell on a different syllable: *e.g. promúlgate*—

> I shall promulgate—I fetch my life and being (i. 2. 21).

sécure (iv 1. 72).

(2) Syllables now pronounced were *slurred*:
either at beginning of a line (i. 3. 277); but in full (v. 1. 129).
gentlemen (as an address)—

> Kind gentlemen, let 's go see poor Cassio dress'd.
> (v. 1. 124).

So v. 1. 105, &c.,

> but *gentleman* (three syllables) (v. 1. 115),
> and *gentlemen* (three syllables) (v. 2. 195).

(3) Unemphatic pronouns and prepositions were often run together with adjacent words, forming a single syllable or its equivalent in time. Thus *of*, o' the: o' th sea (ii. 1. 54, &c.); *it*: not only in *'t is*, *'t was*, *on 't*, *with 't*, but as the object of verbs, *e. g.*—

> Is not to leave 't undone, but to keep 't unknown (iii. 3. 204).

Sometimes the contracted and uncontracted forms occur in the same line:

> Be not acknown on 't; I have use for it (iii. 3. 319).

(4) Conversely, syllables now slurred were pronounced: *búsiness* (three syllables) (i. 1. 154), but scanned as two syllables in i. 2. 90.
The most important example of this kind is the ending *-tion*, *-sion*, still often of two syllables. Its pronunciation and scansion as the equivalent of one syllable was, however, rapidly growing. It becomes steadily more frequent in Shakespeare himself as his career advances. At the date of *Othello* the fuller scansion is practically confined to the last foot of the line, *e.g.*:

> But some uncleanly apprehen | sions | (iii. 3. 139).
> Of law and course of direct ses | sion (i. 2. 86).
> What shall I say? Where's satisfaction? (iii. 3. 401).

But the more archaic practice survives in

> It were an honest act | ion | to say (ii. 3. 146).

The monosyllabic scansion is illustrated on every page, *e.g.*:

> Keep leets and lawdays and | in sess | ion sit |
> Put into circumscrip | tion and | confine (i. 2. 27),

and at the end of the line—

> The wealthy curled darlings of our na | tion (i. 2. 68).
> But this denoted a foregone conclu | sion (iii. 3. 428).

Similarly trisyllabic are *patience* (ii. 3. 376), *signior* (i. 3. 76; iv. 1. 233).
So in names: Cassio is usually scanned with two syllables, but can have three. Cf.:

> How now, good Cassio, what 's the news with you?
>> (iii. 4. 109).

with

> I will not leave him now till Cassio (iii. 4. 32).

Similarly, *Roderigo*, usually scanned as three syllables, has four in v. 2. 113.

2. METRE

1. The *norm* of English blank verse is a line of five metrical beats, separated in pronunciation by equal intervals of time.

The simplest representation of the norm is a verse in which the five beats fall upon five naturally-stressed syllables, the interval preceding each being filled by five syllables without stress.

Such verses occur occasionally in *Othello*; *e.g.*:

> And I 'll devise a mean to draw the Moor (iii. 1. 39)

But the sequence of five metrical beats can be satisfied in many other ways, just as in music an infinity of tunes comply with a given rhythmic basis. And in verse, too, the beauty lies in the new groupings of sound discovered by the melodic instinct of the poet. Almost everything that enters into verse—number of syllables, number of stresses, degree of stress—is variable, provided the sense of metrical sequence is maintained. Thus a verse can have a stress on every syllable, or on no more than four, or even three, as in Shelley's

> Úndulate with the úndulating tíde.

And it can have more than one unstressed syllable, not only, as here, between the stresses, but between the metrical beats.

2. But further, in the verse of Elizabethan drama, including Shakespeare, not only are the musical varieties played on the norm inexhaustible; the norm itself is often relaxed or suspended; in other words, an approach is made to the freedom of conversation; a natural, though not necessary (and in other schools of drama very unusual), characteristic of dramatic dialogue. Thus Shakespeare constantly admits verses both shorter and longer than the norm, and quite incapable of being reduced to it. It is certain that both dramatic realism and joy in the endless wealth of his musical invention had their part in determining the form and character of his verse. But the attempt to discriminate between the two formative influences is for the most part impracticable.

3. NORMAL VARIATIONS

(i) *Extra Syllables*

The normal "decasyllabic" verse was never, in English, strictly limited to ten syllables. At the outset, in Chaucer, the unstressed extra syllable at the end (feminine ending) even predominated, as it did in Italian, where the verse was thence more accurately called "eleven-syllabled" (endecasillabo). And beside that, Chaucer could put two unstressed syllables for one, and even drop the unstressed syllable of the first foot, producing verses of nine, and even twelve, syllables, as well as eleven and ten. In other words, the native tradition of a constant number of stresses survives in him along with the French tradition of a constant number of syllables; and each tradition supplements and modifies the other.

The first blank verse was severely decasyllabic, as in Surrey's *Æneid* and in *Gorboduc*. A great advance towards variety of verse music was made, when this rigor came to be relaxed, in two ways, (1) by the recovery of the Chaucerian unstressed final (eleventh) syllable, (2) by the reassertion of the native (and also classical) tradition of *equivalence*.

In its simplest form this appears in the substitution of a foot (x x —') for (x —'): this is common everywhere in Shakespeare, but, like all other forms of metrical emancipation, gains ground as he advances. This is found (1) within a word or clause:

To take the saf | est occás | ion by the front (iii. 1. 52).
This fort | ificát | ion, gentlemen, shall we see 't? (iii. 2. 5).
Or sue to you and do | a pecu | liar profit (iii. 3. 79).

Similarly *unbonneted* (i. 2. 23), *speculative* (i. 3. 271), &c.
(2) Before a strong pause, especially at the close of a speech:

Nor set down aught in mal | ice: then must you speak
                                                    (v. 2. 343).
Will shake this isl | and.
Mon.   But is he often thus? (ii. 3. 133.)
And that would woo | her. Upon this hint I spake (i. 3. 166).

Even *two extra unstressed syllables* may thus be introduced. While the single unstressed final syllable (feminine ending) is found in all periods of Shakespeare's work, in all his later verse, his hypermetrical unstressed syllables are admitted, not only at the end, but within the line, usually before a pause (i) at the end:

Awáy, I sáy, go óut, and crý a mút || iny.   (iii. 3, 156).
But with a knave of common hire, a gond || olier (i. 1. 126).

(ii) Within the line:

As thóu | dost rúm || inate, and gíve | thy wórst | of thóughts
(iii. 3. 132).
And sóld | to sláv || ery, of mý | redemp | tion thénce.
(i. 3, 138).

(ii) *Variation in the Pauses*

Language, in verse, is a succession of sounds which arrange themselves spontaneously for us in two distinct series of groups:

(1) *Sense* groups—clauses, sentences.
(2) *Metrical* groups—feet, verses.

The earliest English blank verse tended to make these groups
coincide, and this tendency is still very perceptible in the early
verse of Shakespeare, as in that of Marlowe.

But as he advances he tends more and more to make the groups
not coincide but overlap. A growing proportion of sentences, and
a smaller, but also growing, proportion of clauses, end within the
verse, not at its close. An important case of the first is the speech-
endings, which also, it is found, increasingly occur within the verse.
While the "weak" or "light" ending, where a single clause flows
over, without any grammatical pause, from one verse to the next,
becomes the most striking characteristic of his later metrical style.
It is traceable, but not yet largely developed, in *Othello*.

Light endings, *e.g.*:

> It were an honest action to say
> So to the Moor (ii. 3. 146).

> That by your virtuous means I may again
> Exist (iii. 4. 111).

(iii) *Variations in Stress*

The greatest source of flexibility in Elizabethan verse lies in the
endless modulations of stress. While quantity, in classical measures,
is either short or long, stress may have an indefinite number of
subtle gradations, and, provided that the five beats of the normal
verse are sustained, or not overpowered, any degree of stress is admissible in any place. Thus, while the average verse has four main
stresses, a verse made of a succession of monosyllables may have
eight or nine, as in Milton's:

> Rocks, Caves, Lakes, Fens, Bogs, Dens, and shades of death.
> > (*Paradise Lost*, ii. 621).

And many verses of great beauty have three, *e.g.*:

> And smóoth as monuméntal alabáster (v. 2. 5).

Hence we find in the same foot all gradations from $(-'\ -')$ to $(x\ x)$, for the metrical beat either concurs with the stress or takes its place. Even the inversion $(-\ x)$ of the normal foot is not only admissible but of great beauty and constant occurrence, for the traversing of the normal rhythm, followed by its recovery, has the charm of a discord in music, immediately resolved. Whereas a succession of five such feet would wholly change the character of the line, compelling us to refer it to another norm. Such a verse, indeed, we have in Lear's:

> Never, never, never, never, never.

But this is rather to be regarded as one of the countless dramatic departures from the norm than as a variation of it.

The possible variations in stress in a single Shakespearean verse are thus infinite, and could only be registered by a far finer notation than is at our disposal. It must suffice to give examples of the most marked and salient cases.

(1) Feet without stress. Especially common at the end of the line:

> O insupportable! O heavy hour! (v. 2. 98).
> Steep'd me in pov | erty to | the very lips (iv. 2. 50).
> But to know so must be my bén | efit (iii. 4. 119).

(2) Feet with double stress. This is often combined with (i) forming a figure of great beauty, particularly common in Milton. *E.g.*:

> Thy match was mortal to | him, and púre gríef (v. 2. 205)
> Lead to the Sagittary the raísed seárch (i. 1. 159).

(3) Feet with *inverted* stress. This also forms with a following normal foot a figure of great beauty. In the first foot it is frequent in all periods. In the fourth foot, also, it is common in all periods of Shakespeare:

> In this time of the night! | Bríng him | awáy! (i. 2. 94).

It is less common in the third:

> Have I to-night | flústered | with flów | ing cups (ii. 3. 60).

So ii. 3. 64;

and rare in the second and fifth. A possible example is:

> Stay ye, good gent | lemen. Look | you pále, | mistress?
> (v. 1. 105)

4. ABNORMAL VARIATIONS

But many verses are found, as already stated (iii. 2), in all Shake-speare's mature work, which cannot be referred to the norm at all. The general explanation being that dramatic truth has got the better of metrical fidelity, and to that extent deflected the verse from the norm. Almost all these verses occur where continuity is interrupted by a strong pause; especially by the division between two speeches.

(i) The verse is abnormally long. We often find verses, nominally of six feet, forming two phrases of three feet each.

(*a*) Within the same speech:

> Richer than all his tribe; | of one whose subdued eyes,
> (v. 2. 348).

> As my young mistress' dog. | Now, my sick fool Roderigo
> (ii. 3. 53).

(*b*) Between two speeches:

> *Des.* To-morrow dinner, then?
> *Oth.* I shall not dine at home.

(ii) The verse is abnormally short. Here the two phrases form a line of less than normal length:

> Must be to loathe her. O curse of marriage (iii. 3. 268).
> More than their own. What then? how then? (iii. 3. 400).
> Made to write "whore" upon? What committed? (iv. ii. 72).
> That married with Othello. You, mistress (iv. ii. 90).

(iii) Such short lines, mostly of three, but also of two and of four, often occur alone.

(1) At the close of a speech; especially where the following speech is not directly in reply to the first:

> [*Sailor*]. By Signior Angelo.
> *Duke* [*to the Senators*]. How say you by this change? &c.

So Iago's comment, which Othello ignores, upon Othello's anguished outburst (iii. 3. 338 *f*.; i. 3. 17):

> I am sorry to hear this (iii. 3. 344).

So iv. 32 and 64 below, 127, 172, 192, &c. Or Othello's slow, pon-
dering

> Certain, men should be what they seem (iii. 3. 128).

(2) Within the speech:

> *Oth.*   . . . the battles, sieges, fortunes,
>   That I have pass'd (i. 3. 131).

So Iago, prefacing his labored "praise" of Desdemona (ii. 1. 129)
and his account of "Cassio's dream" (iii. 3. 415–19).

Moments of peculiar intensity may even produce complete dislocation of verse-structure, an occasional fragment of metre alone
preserving the continuity of impression which would be broken by
a definite descent to prose.

Thus the dialogue of Othello and Iago in iii. 3. 100 *f*.:

> *Iago.* Indeed!
> *Oth.* Indeed! ay, indeed: discern'st thou aught in that?
> Is he not honest?
> *Iago.*   Honest, my lord!
> *Oth.* Honest, ay, honest!
> *Iago.*   My lord, for aught I know.
> *Oth.* What dost thou think?
> *Iago.*   Think, my lord?
> *Oth.* Think, my lord! By heaven, he echoes me, &c.

There is similar dislocation in the crucial dialogue of Othello and
Desdemona in iii. 4. 80 *f*., and in the night brawl v. 1. 40 *f*.

No sharp line can be drawn in practice between the normal verses
with two extra unstressed syllables, discussed in iii. 3 above, and
the abnormal verses of six feet. Nor, again, can we wholly reject
the view that in some of the "short" verses Shakespeare may have
scanned a strongly-emphatic syllable as a foot. But since verses
abound which cannot possibly be explained in this way, it is hazardous to rely upon it in any. As to the long verses, it must suffice
to recognize that verses of twelve syllables may arise in two ways—
by a complication of the normal verse, and by a definite infringe-
ment of the norm—and that in a large number of cases the two
types thence arising can be distinguished.

APPENDIX II

THE TIME–RELATIONS

No reader or hearer who gives himself up to the overwhelming impression of the tragic action is likely to ask within what limits of time it is supposed to happen. But closer scrutiny shows, as has long been noticed, that this question cannot be confidently answered; not because it is left obscure, but because two wholly inconsistent answers can be gathered from the text. The latest and most critical discussion of the question is that of Dr. A. C. Bradley, *Shakespearean Tragedy*, Note I, upon which the following statement of the facts is based. Cf. also the account of previous discussions in Furness's Variorum edition of the play, p. 338 *f.*

Two sets of time indications may be found in the play. According to the first (which we may conveniently call A), Desdemona was murdered, at most a few days, and most probably on the night but one, after her arrival at Cyprus. According to the second, (B), an interval of some weeks intervened.

Taking A first. On the night following the arrival of Othello, Desdemona, and Cassio—in different ships—at Cyprus, occurs the brawl and Cassio's dismissal (ii. 3). He resolves to ask Desdemona's intercession "betimes in the morning" (ii. 3. 335).

In Act iii. 3 he does so, and Desdemona intercedes. In the same scene Iago begins to poison Othello's mind, with the result that, at the close, *i.e.* still on the day following the arrival, he orders the death of Cassio and prepares to murder Desdemona. The handkerchief has already been lost, and taken by Iago, and Iago has already insinuated that he has seen Cassio using it. In iii. 4 Othello inquires for the handkerchief, and after his departure Cassio is accosted by Bianca.

Act iv. 1 must follow at once, since Bianca is said to have had the handkerchief from Cassio "even now" (v. 155). She here invites him to supper *to-night*. In iv. 2 Iago persuades Roderigo to kill Cassio as he comes from supper with her *to-night*. In v. 1, Emilia rushes in with the news of this assault, immediately after the death of Desdemona.

From all this it appears hard to escape from the conclusion that only one day separates Desdemona's union with Othello and her murder.

On the other hand, a number of the passages (B) imply that a longer time—some weeks, at least—has elapsed. Thus Bianca has had time not only to make Cassio's acquaintance, but to pall on him and be neglected; she complains that he has been absent eight days; yet, according to ii. 1, Cassio only arrived at Cyprus on the morning of Othello's arrival, *i.e.* a day and a half, at most, before. Similarly, Iago speaks of having slept with Cassio and heard his profession of love to Desdemona. This is naturally a lie; but how can Othello accept it if Cassio had passed only a single night at Cyprus—the night of his own union with Desdemona—as A requires? And, above all, Othello repeatedly uses language which implies that he believes his wife's offence with Cassio to have been many times committed (v. 2. 210), and he bitterly reflects on his happiness in not knowing it—"I slept the next night well" (iii. 3. 340), when "the next night" after the first possible commission of the offence is still to come—the night in which he will put her to death? To these may be added the difficulty of explaining the recall of Othello —which no one in the play appears to think strange—on the day following his arrival to assume the command. Similarly, Roderigo, who at the close of Act i resolves to sell his land in order to woo Desdemona with the proceeds, has "almost spent" his money on the night following his arrival in Cyprus (ii. 3. 371). He certainly speaks as if he had been there some time.

It must suffice here to mention the three principal hypotheses which have been advanced to meet the case.

(1) Desdemona's offence is supposed to have occurred before marriage. This is favored by Iago's question, in iii. 3, as to Cassio's knowledge of the courtship, and by Othello's insult (iv. 2. 89), but is inconsistent with Othello's belief that she is false to *him*, and would greatly weaken the force of the whole. Nor does it relieve the time difficulties relating to Bianca and to the Venetian envoys.

(2) Our text was first published in 1622, six years after Shakespeare's death. It is suggested that it may have been curtailed for acting purposes, and that a scene may have been excised which introduced an interval of some weeks between the landing (ii. 1) and the brawl (ii. 3). This would remove most of the difficulties, but requires the excision of several passages which imply that the brawl happened on the night following the landing.

(3) It is supposed that Shakespeare deliberately admitted two scales of time (called by "Christopher North," who first suggested this, "short time" and "long time"), as if thus gaining at once the effect of the terrific swiftness of the main action and yet retaining the rationality of the minor circumstances. The example of the

Merchant of Venice, where time at Venice and at Belmont do not tally, prevents our absolutely rejecting this possibility. It could be only an extension of the ideal treatment of time (and space) presupposed in the whole Elizabethan drama to imagine a different time-rate in different parts of the action. But the trouble here is that the main action itself cannot have this "terrific swiftness" without becoming irrational, and therefore at bottom unintelligible.

Perhaps, in the last resort, we may find a clue in this very fact, and recognize that, as in genius itself there is something which our rationality sees as unreason, so the overwhelming imaginative effect of a supreme poem may be brought about by processes which, when we try to analyze them, fall apart into discrepant elements, like the divergent visual images which the stereoscope blends into one harmonious vision. Whether carelessness, as modern criticism tends to believe, or profound calculation, as North and his generation held, was the source of these and similar discrepancies, the central and salient fact for us is that when *Othello* is read or seen with an imagination fully kindled and alert, these discrepancies are not felt, because such an imagination becomes absorbed and possessed by the overpowering tragic situation itself, to the eternal truth of which time and place are at the bottom irrelevant. The cool analytic scrutiny which discovers them sees justly, but it is not to this temper that poetry is addressed or to which it discloses its inmost secrets.

APPENDIX III

SHAKESPEARE'S STAGE IN ITS BEARING
UPON HIS DRAMA

1. The structure and arrangement of the Elizabethan theater are still under discussion, and many points of detail remain unsettled. The last twenty years have produced a very extensive and highly technical literature on the subject, chiefly in England, America, and Germany. It is based especially on the new evidence derived from (1) the original stage directions, and (2) contemporary illustrations and descriptions. The following summary gives the conclusions which at present appear most reasonable, neglecting much speculative matter of great interest.

2. When Shakespeare arrived in London, soon after 1585, theatrical exhibitions were given there in (1) public theaters, (2) private theaters, (3) the halls of the royal palaces, and of the Inns of Court.

Of the "public" theaters there were at least three: The Theater, the Curtain, both in Shoreditch, and Newington Butts on the Bankside or Southwark shore. About 1587, the Rose, also on the Bankside, was added. All these were occasionally used by Shakespeare's company before 1599, when their headquarters became the newly built Globe, likewise on the Bankside. Of the "private" theaters the principal, and the oldest, was the Blackfriars, on the site of the present *Times* office. It was also the property of the company in which Shakespeare acquired a share, but being let out during practically his whole career, does not count in the present connection. At court, on the other hand, his company played repeatedly. But his plays were written for the "public" theater, and this alone had influence upon his stage-craft.

3. The "public" theater differed from the other two types chiefly in being (1) dependent on daylight, (2) open overhead, and (3) partially seatless; and from the court-stages also, in (4) not using painted scenes. While they, again, had the rectangular form, the typical "public" theater was a round or octagonal edifice, modelled partly on the inn-yards where companies of players had been accustomed to perform, prior to the inhibition of 1574, on movable stages;

partly on the arenas used for bear-baiting and cock-fighting—sports still carried on in the theaters, and in part dictating their arrangements.

The circular inner area, known thence as the cock-pit, or pit, had accordingly no seats; admission to it cost one penny (6*d*. in modern money), and the standing spectators were known as the "groundlings." More expensive places (up to 2*s*. 6*d*.) with seats, were provided in tiers of galleries which ran round the area, one above the other, as in modern theaters; the uppermost being covered with a thatched roof.

4. THE STAGE (using the term to describe the entire scenic apparatus of the theater) included (1) the *outer stage*, a rectangular platform (as much as 42 feet wide in the largest examples) projecting into the circular area, from the back wall, and thus surrounded by "groundlings" on three sides. Above it were a thatched roof and hangings, but no side or front curtains. In the floor was a trapdoor by which ghosts and others ascended or descended. At the back were (2) two projecting wings, each with a door opening obliquely on to the stage, the *recess* between them, of uncertain shape and extent, forming a kind of inner stage. Above this was (3) an upper room or rooms, which included the actors' "tiring-house," with a window or windows opening on (4) a *balcony* or gallery, from which was hung (5) a *curtain*, by means of which the inner recess could be concealed or disclosed.

5. The most important divergence of this type of structure from that of our theaters is in the relation between the outer stage and the auditorium. In the modern theater the play is treated as a picture, framed in the proscenium arch, seen by the audience like any other picture from the front only, and shut off from their view at any desired moment by letting the curtain fall. An immediate consequence of this was that a scene (or act) could terminate only in one of two ways. Either the persons concerned in it walked, or were carried, off the stage; or a change of place and circumstances was *supposed* without their leaving it. Both these methods were used. The first was necessary only at the close of the play. For this reason an Elizabethan play rarely ends on a *climax*, such as the close of Ibsen's *Ghosts;* the overpowering effect of which would be gravely diminished, if instead of the curtain falling upon Oswald's helpless cry for "the sun," he and his mother had to walk off the stage. Marlowe's *Faustus* ends with a real climax, because the catastrophe *ipso facto* leaves the stage clear. But the close of even the most overwhelming final scenes of Shakespeare is relatively

quiet, or even, as in *Macbeth*, a little tame. The concluding lines often provide a motive for the (compulsory) clearing of the stage.

In the *Tragedies*, the dead body of the hero has usually to be borne ceremoniously away, followed by the rest; so Aufidius in *Coriolanus*: "Help, three o' the chiefest soldiers; I'll be one." Similarly in *Hamlet* and *King Lear*. In *Othello*, Desdemona's bed was apparently in the curtained recess, and at the close the curtains were drawn upon the two bodies, instead of their being as usual borne away.

The close of the *Histories* often resembles the dispersing of an informal council after a declaration of policy by the principal person; thus *Richard II* closes with Bolingbroke's announcement of the penance he proposes to pay for Richard's death; *Henry IV* with his orders for the campaign against Northumberland and Glendower; *King John* with Falconbridge's great assertion of English patriotism.

In the *Comedies*, the leading persons will often withdraw to explain to one another at leisure what the audience already knows (*Winter's Tale*, *Tempest*, *Merchant of Venice*), or to carry out the wedding rites (*As You Like It*, *Midsummer-Night's Dream*); or they strike up a measure and thus (as in *Much Ado*) naturally dance off the stage. Sometimes the chief persons have withdrawn before the close, leaving some minor character—Puck (*Midsummer-Night's Dream*) or the Clown (*Twelfth Night*)—to wind up the whole with a snatch of song, and then retire himself.

6. But the most important result of the exposed stage was that it placed strict limits upon dramatic illusion, and thus compelled the resort, for most purposes, to conventions resting on symbolism, suggestion, or make-believe. It was only in dress that anything like simulation could be attempted; and here the Elizabethan companies, as is well known, were lavish in the extreme. Painted scenes, on the other hand, even had they been available, would have been idle or worse, when perhaps a third of the audience would see, behind the actors, not the scenes but the people in the opposite gallery, or the gallants seated on the stage. Especially where complex and crowded actions were introduced, the most beggarly symbolic suggestion was cheerfully accepted. Jonson, in the spirit of classicist realism, would have tabooed all such intractable matter; and he scoffed, in his famous Prologue, at the "three rusty swords" whose clashing had to do duty for "York and Lancaster's long jars." Shakespeare's realism was never of this literal kind, but in bringing Agincourt upon the stage of the newly built Globe in the following year (1599) he showed himself so far sensitive to criticisms of this type that he expressly appealed to the audience's imagination—

"eke out our imperfections with your thoughts"—consenting, more-over, to assist them by the splendid descriptive passages interposed between the Acts.

It is probable that the Elizabethan popular audience did not need any such appeal. It had no experience of elaborate realism on the stage; the rude movable stages on which the earliest dramas had been played compelled an ideal treatment of *space* and a symbolic treatment of *properties;* and this tradition, though slowly giving way, was still paramount throughout Shakespeare's career. Thus every audience accepted as a matter of course (1) the representation of *distant* things or places simultaneously on the stage. Sidney, in 1580, had 'ridiculed the Romantic plays of his time with "Asia of one side and Africa of the other," indicated by labels. But Shake-speare in 1593-4 could still represent the tents of Richard III and Richmond within a few yards of one another, and the Ghosts speak-ing alternately to each. Every audience accepted (2) the presence on the stage, in full view of the audience, of accessories irrelevant to the scene in course of performance. A property requisite for one set of scenes, but out of place in another, could be simply ignored while the latter were in progress; just as the modern audience sees but never reckons as scenery, the footlights and the prompter's box. Large, movable objects, such as beds or chairs, were no doubt often brought in when needed; but no one was disturbed if they remained during an intervening scene in which they were out of place. And "properties either difficult to move, like a well, or so small as to be unobtrusive, were habitually left on the stage as long as they were wanted, whatever scenes intervened" (Reynolds).

Thus in Jonson's *The Case is Altered* (an early play, not yet re-flecting his characteristic technique), Jaques, in iii. 2, hides his gold in the earth and covers it with a heap of dung to avoid sus-picion. In iv. 4, he removes the dung to assure himself that the gold is still there. The intervening scenes represent rooms in Fer-neze's palace, and Juniper's shop; but the heap of dung doubtless remained on the stage all the time. Similarly in Peele's *David and Bethsabe*, the spring in which Bethsabe bathes; and in his *Old Wives' Tale*, a "study" and a "cross," which belong to unconnected parts of the action.

It follows from this that the *supposed locality of a scene could be changed* without any change in the properties on the stage, or even of the persons. What happened was merely that some properties which previously had no dramatic relevance, suddenly acquired it, and *vice versa;* that a tree, for instance, hitherto only a stage property out of use, became a *tree* and signified probably, a wood. The change of scene may take place without any break in the dialogue, and be marked only by the occurrence of allusions of a different tenor.

Thus in *Doctor Faustus*, at v. 1106 *f.*, Faustus is in "a fair and pleasant green," on his way from the Emperor's Court to Wittenberg; at v. 1143 *f.*, he is back in his house there. In *Romeo and Juliet*, i. 4. 5, Romeo and his friends are at first in the street; at i. 4, 114, according to the Folio, "they march about the stage and servingmen come forth with their napkins"; in other words, we are now in Capulet's hall, and Capulet presently enters, meeting his guests. This is conventionalized in modern editions.

7. THE INNER STAGE.—An audience for which the limitations of the actual stage meant so little, might be expected to dispense readily with the concessions to realism implied in providing an actual inner chamber for scenes performed "within," and an actual gallery for those performed "aloft." And the importance and number of the former class of scenes has, in fact, been greatly exaggerated.

Applying modern usages to the semi-medieval Elizabethan stage, Brandl (*Einleitung* to his revised edition of Schlegel's translation) and Brodmeier (Dissertation on the Stage-conditions of the Elizabethan Drama), put forward the theory of the "alternative" scene; according to which the inner and the outer stage were used "alternately," a recurring scene, with elaborate properties, being arranged in the former, and merely curtained off while intervening scenes were played on the outer, or main stage. But while this theory is plausible, as applied to some of Shakespeare's plays (*e. g.* the intricate transitions between rooms at Belmont and piazzas at Venice, in the *Merchant*), it breaks down in others (*e. g. Cymbeline*, ii. 2, 3; *Richard II*, i. 3, 4), and especially in many plays by other dramatists.

It is probable that the use of the "inner stage" was in general restricted to two classes of scene: (1) where persons "within" formed an integral though subordinate part of a scene of which the main issue was decided on the outer stage; as with the play-scene in *Hamlet*, or where Ferdinand and Miranda are discovered playing chess in *The Tempest;* (2) where a scene, though engaging the whole interest, is supposed to occur in an inner chamber. Thus Desdemona's chamber, Prospero's cell, Timon's cave, Lear's hovel, the Capulets' tomb.

8. THE BALCONY.—There is less doubt about the use of the balcony or gallery. This was in fact an extremely favorite resource, and its existence in part explains the abundance of serenade, rope-ladder, and other upper-story scenes in Elizabethan drama.

From the balcony, or the window above it, Juliet discoursed with Romeo, and Sylvia with Proteus (*Two Gentlemen of Verona*, iv. 2); Richard III addressed the London citizens, and the citizen of Angers the rival Kings. From the window the Pedant in *Taming of the Shrew*, v. 1, hails Petruchio and Grumio below; and Squire Tub, in Jonson's *Tale of a Tub*, i. 1, puts out his head in answer to the summons of Parson Hugh. But whole scenes were also, it is probable, occasionally enacted in this upper room. This is the most natural interpretation of the scenes in Juliet's chamber (iv. 3, 5). On the other hand, though the Senators in *Titus Andronicus*, i. 1, "go up into the Senate House," it is probable that the debate later in the scene, on the main stage, is intended to be in the Senate House by the convention described in 6.

For further reference the following among others may be mentioned:—

G. F. Reynolds, *Some Principles of Elizabethan Staging* (*Modern Philology*, II. iii.); A. Brandl, *Introduction* to his edition of Schlegel's translation of Shakespeare; V. E. Albright, *The Shakespearian Stage* (New York); W. Archer, *The Elizabethan Stage* (*Quarterly Review* 1908); W. J. Lawrence, *The Elizabethan Playhouse and other Studies* (1st and 2d series); D. Figgis, *Shakespeare, a Study*.

From one or other of these, many of the above examples have been taken.

C. H. H.

GLOSSARY

abused (iii. 3. 200), deceived.

addition (iii. 4. 194), honor; (iv. 2. 163, &c.), title.

advantage (iii. 3. 212), favorable opportunity.

affined (i. 1. 39), bound in obligation.

affinity (iii. 1. 49), family relationship.

agnize (i. 3. 232), acknowledge.

aim (i. 3. 6), conjecture, guess.

Almain (ii. 3. 86), German.

ancient (i. 1. 33. and *passim*), a phonetic corruption for ensign.

antres (i. 3. 140), caverns.

approve (ii. 3. 316), find by trial, prove; cf. ii. 3. 211. Also to accept, credit (as likely to be found true if tried, like L. *probabilis*) (i. 3. 11).

aspic (iii. 3. 450), asp.

attack (i. 2. 77), arrest.

be-leed (i. 1. 30), left in the lee, passed by like a ship becalmed.

besort (i. 3. 239), company.

bob (v. 1. 16), procure cunningly in order to defraud.

by (i. 3. 17), about, concerning. Cf. Abbott, § 145.

callet (iv. 2. 121), cant term for "mistress."

capable (iii. 3. 458), comprehensive.

carack (i. 2. 50), merchant-vessel (and so likely to have a rich cargo).

cast (i. 1. 150; ii. 3. 14. 273), cast off, dismiss.

censure (ii. 3. 193, &c.), judgment.

challenge (ii. 1. 213), claim.

chamberer (iii. 3. 265), drawing-room knight, courtier.

chrysolite (v. 2. 145), a green jewel.

civil (iv. 1. 65), citizen (as adjective).

clip (iii. 3. 464), embrace.

cog (iv. 2. 132), cheat.

collied (ii. 3. 206), obscured.

commoner (iv. 2. 73), prostitute.

condition (ii. 1. 255; iv. 1. 204), disposition, character.

consul (i. 1. 25; 2. 43), counsellor (in the Grand Council of Venice).

continuate (iii. 4. 178), uninterrupted.

convinced (iv. 1. 28), overcome.

corrigible (i. 3. 329), corrective.

counter-caster (i. 1. 31), clerk (one who uses counters in book-keeping).

country (adj.) (iii. 3. 201, 237), native.

daff (iv. 2. 176), put off.

dear (i. 3. 85), intense, zealous, extreme.

demerit (i. 2. 22), merit. Minsheu Dict., 1621: *demerite*, a desert.

dilate (i. 3. 153), relate at large. Cf. *Com. Err.* (i. 1. 123), "dilate at full what hath befallen of them."

dispose (i. 3. 403), disposition.

doubt (iii. 3. 19), suspect.

ecstasy (iv. 1. 80), madness; hence, a fit.

engines (iv. 2. 221), plots.

ensteeped (ii. 1. 70), immersed deep in water.

escape (i. 3. 197), escapade.

favour (ii. 1. 232), countenance.

fineless (iii. 3. 173), endless, infinite.

fitchew (iv. 1. 150), a pole-cat.

174

fond (i. 3. 320), foolish.
fop (iv. 2. 198), make a fool of.
fordo (v. 1. 129), undo, ruin.
fraught (iii. 3. 449), burden.
free (ii. 3, 343), frank, sincere. So *freely* (ii. 3. 324, &c.).
frize (ii. 1. 127), coarse woollen stuff.
from (i. 1. 132), contrary to.
front (i. 3. 80; iii. 1. 52), forehead.

gender (iv. 2. 62), engender, multiply.
generous (iii. 3. 280), noble, well-born.
gennets (i. 1. 114), Moorish horses.
germans (i. 1. 114), relatives.
grange (i. 1. 107), an outlying farmhouse.
grise (i. 3. 200), flight of steps.
guardage (i. 2. 70), guarded safety.

happily (iii. 3. 238), haply.

idle (i. 3. 140), unoccupied, empty.
import (iii. 3. 317), importance.
incontinent (iv. 3. 12), immediately.
ingener (ii. 1. 65), inventor, contriver.
injointed (i. 3. 35), joined.
intentively (i. 3. 155), with mind bent upon the matter; attentively.

jump (i. 3. 5), agree.

lay (ii. 3. 330), wager.
liberal (ii. 1. 165), licentious.

mammering (iii. 3. 70), hesitating.
manure (i. 3. 328), till, cultivate.
mazzard (ii. 3. 156), head.
mere (ii. 2. 3), total.
moe (iv. 3. 57), more (orig. neuter form of the comparative, used of numbers).
mortal (ii. 1. 72), deadly, destructive.
motion (i. 2. 76), apprehension; (i. 3. 95, 335), impulse.

night-gown (iv. 3. 34), a loose cloak or dressing-gown, which could be worn out of doors.
nonsuits (i. 1. 16), dismisses as having no case, the most humiliating form of defeat in the law courts.

notorious (iv. 2. 140; v. 2. 239), egregious.

opinion (ii. 3. 195), reputation.
opposite (i. 2. 67), averse, opposed.
owe (i. 1. 66, &c.), own, possess.

paragon (ii. 1. 62), serve as a pattern for, excel.
perdition (ii. 2. 3), loss, destruction.
perdurable (i. 3. 343), enduring.
pioner (iii. 3. 346), miner.
pliant (i. 3. 151) (of time), disposable, free.
poise (iii. 3. 82), weight.
portance (i. 3. 139), bearing.
potting (ii. 3. 79), drinking.
pottle-deep (ii. 3. 56), to the bottom of the measure (of two quarts).
practice (v. 2. 292), insidious plot.
pregnant (ii. 1. 239), evident.
probal (ii. 3. 344), plausible.
proper (i. 3. 69, 265), own, personal.
proper (iv. 3. 35), handsome.

quarter (ii. 3. 180), concord.
quat (v. 1. 11), pimple.
quillet (iii. 1. 25), quibble.
quirks (ii. 1. 63), flourishes.

raise (i. 1. 159, &c.), rouse, call up, awaken.
recognizance (v. 2. 214), token.
remorse (iii. 3. 369), pity.
repeal (ii. 3. 363), recall.
rheum (iii. 4. 51), discharge from eyes or nose.
round (i. 3. 90), straightforward, direct.
rouse (ii. 3. 67), a large draught, a bumper.

salt (ii. 1. 244), licentious.
sect (i. 3. 336), cutting, sprout.
seel (i. 3. 270), blind, blindfold (in falconry).
sentence (i. 3. 199), a gnomic or proverbial saying. Hence "sententious."
sequent (i. 2. 41), successive.
siege (i. 2. 22) [L. *sedes*], place, rank; from the *seats* set in order of precedence at table.
signiory (i. 2. 18), the Grand Council of Venice.
skillet (i. 3. 273), kettle.

slipper (ii. 1. 246), slippery, crafty.
slubber (i. 3. 227), soil, dim.
splinter (ii. 3. 329), put between splints.
stomach (v. 2. 75), appetite.

theoric (i. 1. 24), theoretical knowledge.
traverse (i. 3. 379), a military command, step out, go.

undertaker (iv. 1. 223), one who represents or takes the part of another.
use (iv. 1. 285; iv. 3. 105), custom, habit.
usurped (i. 3. 345), false.

vicious (iii. 3. 145), erroneous.

yerk'd (i. 2. 5), struck, stabbed. A phonetic variant for "jerked."